ASSIGNMENTS IN

BRITISH SOCIAL & ECONOMIC HISTORY

ASSIGNMENTS IN
BRITISH SOCIAL & ECONOMIC HISTORY

Nicholas Tate

Nelson

Thomas Nelson and Sons Ltd
Nelson House Mayfield Road
Walton-on-Thames Surrey
KT12 5PL UK

51 York Place
Edinburgh
ED1 3JD UK

Thomas Nelson (Hong Kong) Ltd
Toppan Building 10/F
22A Westlands Road
Quarry Bay Hong Kong

Distributed in Australia by

Thomas Nelson Australia
480 La Trobe Street
Melbourne Victoria 3000
and in Sydney, Brisbane, Adelaide and Perth

First published by Thomas Nelson and Sons Ltd 1989

ISBN 0-17-445171-7

NPN 9 8 7 6 5 4 3 2 1

Printed and bound in Hong Kong

Acknowledgements

The author and publishers are grateful to the following for permission to reproduce copyright material .

Photographs and cartoons

The Architectural Review (p. 123) BBC Enterprises (p. 139 *both*) Bedford School (p.121) A. Ronald Brelby (p.137) The British Library (pp. 12 *top*, 26, 89 *both*, 122 *bottom*) British Steel Corporation (p.100 *right*) Roy Brook (pp. 58 *all*, 59) His Grace the Duke of Buccleuch and Queensberry (p.16 *top*) Cambridge University Collection of Air Photographs (p. 17) J. Allan Cash Ltd (pp. 31, 35, 49) Mary Evans/Fawcett Library (p. 145) *Evening Standard*/Centre for the Study of Cartoons and Caricature, University of Kent at Canterbury (p. 70 *top*) The Fotomas Index (pp. 12 *bottom*, 15, 52, 54, 73, 74 *both*, 94, 127) The Fotomas Index/John R. Freeman (pp. 7, 47) John Gorman (pp. 100 *left*, 101 *top*, 102) Greater London Picture Library (p. 154) Sally & Richard Greenhill (p.153) Hulton-Deutsch Collection (pp. 33 *bottom right*, 109, 117, 119 *top*, 146, 148 *bottom*) Institute of Agricultural History and Museum of English Rural Life, University of Reading (pp. 20 *top and bottom*, 21 *top*) Jackdaw (pp. 92/3) Leeds City Council (p. 7) The Mansell Collection (p. 21 *bottom*, 33 *top left and centre left*, 79) Mary Evans Picture Library (p. 33 *centre left*) *New Statesman* (p. 70 *bottom*) Northampton Local History Library (p. 119 *bottom*) Peek Frean & Co (p. 149) The Press Association Ltd (p. 101 *bottom*) The Royal Commission on the Ancient & Historical Monuments of Scotland (pp. 36 *bottom*, 37) Royal Commission on the Historical Monuments of England (p. 36 *top*) Science Museum (pp. 33 *top right and bottom left*) Shell Photographic Library (p. 39) Solo Syndication and Literary Agency/Centre for the Study of Cartoons and Caricature, University of Kent at Canterbury (p. 112, 133) Topham Picture Library (pp. 107, 148 *top*) Wellcome Institute Library, London (p. 129).

Extracts and Statistics

pp. 8, 9, Cambridge University Press for statistics from B.R. Mitchell and P. Deane, *Abstract of British Historical Statistics*, 1962; pp. 13, 24, 75, 112, The Controller of Her Majesty's Stationery Office for extracts from Parliamentary Papers 1851 XL (198), 1897 XV, 1842 XV, XVII and XVI, 1942–3 VI; p. 18, Hodder & Stoughton for an extract from W.G. Hoskins, *The English Landscape*, 1955; p. 25, *The Economic History Review*, IX(1), 1961; pp. 28, 29, Cambridge University Press for extracts from J. Thirsk, *The Agrarian History of England and Wales VIII 1934–39*, 1978; pp. 40, 41, 42 Macmillan Publishers Ltd for extracts from S.B. Saul, *The Myth of the Great Depression 1873–1896*, 1969; p. 42, Cambridge University Press for an extraxt from W.H.B. Court (ed.), *British Economic History 1870–1914*, 1965; p. 43, Macmillan Publishers Ltd for an extract from N. Tonge & M. Quincey, *British Social and Economic History 1800–1900*, 1980; p. 44, Education for The Industrial Society Project, Scottish Consultative Council on the Curriculum, for an extract from M.S. Moss, *Growth and Decline of Clyde Shipbuilding*, 1986; p. 44, Edward Arnold (Publishers) Ltd for an extract from C. Harvey, *No Gods and Precious Few Heroes: Scotland 1914–1980*, 1981; pp. 45, Corgi for extracts from A. McArthur and H. Kingsley Long, *No mean City*, 1978; pp. 45, Transworld Publishers for an extract from H. Munro, *The Clydesiders*, 1970; pp. 48, 49, 50, 51, B.T. Batsford Ltd for extracts from D.D. Gladwin, *The Waterways of Britain*, 1976; p. 53, The open University Press for an extract from C. Harvey, G. Martin and A. Scharf (eds), *Industrialisation and Culture 1830–1914*, 1970; p. 57, Times Newspapers Ltd for extracts from R.H. Longridge, *Life in the 1870's as Seen through Advertisements in* The Times, 1974; p. 60, 62 Methuen & Co for an extract from J. Curran and J. Seton, *Power and Responsibility. The Press and Broadcasting in Britain,* 1985; p.61, The Controller of Her Majesty's Stationery office for an extract from *Social Trends,* 1982; p.62, Heinemann Professional Publishing Ltd for an extract from S. Hood, *A Survey of Television*, 1967; pp. 67, 76, 131, The Controller of Her Majesty's Stationery Office for extracts from *Hansard*, 1842, 1845, 1946; p. 68 Century Hutchinson Ltd for an extract from D. Holmon (ed.), *Portraits and Documents Earlier 19th Century*, 1965; pp. 82, 83, John Burnett for extracts from *Destiny Obscure*, 1982; p. 86, Heinemann Professional Publishing Ltd for an extract from J.B. Priestley, *English Journey*, 1934; p.87, The estate of Sonia Bronwell Orwell and Secker & Warburg Ltd for an extract from G. Orwell, *The Road to Wigan Pier*; pp. 103, 104, Unwin Hyman Ltd for extracts from R. Page Arnot, *The Miners: Years of Struggle,* 1953; p. 105, Unwin Hyman Ltd for an extract from R.A. Leeson, *Strike: A Live History 1887–1971*, 1973; pp. 109, 110, 111, Methuen & Co for extracts from M.A. Crowther, *The Workhouse System 1834–1929*, 1983; p. 112, Mirror Group Newspapers for an extract from the *Daily Mirror*, 1943; p. 118, Oxford University Press for an extract from K. Dawson and P. Wall, *Society and Industry in the 19th Century, 4. Education*, 1969; p. 118, 119, Routledge Publishers for extracts from M. Seabourne, *Education,* 1966; p. 124, The Controller of Her Majesty's Stationery office for an extract from the *The New Secondary Education*, Ministry of Education Pamphlet No. 9, 1947; p. 132, Heinemann Professional Publishing Ltd for an extract from A. Bevan, *In Place of Fear*, 1952; p. 136, 137, 140, Duckworth & Co Ltd for extracts from J. Gray, *The Geography of Religion*, 1971; p. 139, BBC Enterprises for an extract from the *Radio Times*, 1988; p.142, The Open University Press for an extract from F. Galton, *Memories of My Life*, Arts Foundation Course 1987; p. 150, Macmillan Publishers Ltd for an extract from D.C. Brooks, *The Emancipation of Women*, 1970; p. 150, Jonathan Cape Ltd for an extract from A. Calder, *The People's War*; p. 150, The Open University Press for an extract from the Third Level Course: War and Society (World War II); p. 157, Yorkshire Post Newspapers Ltd for an extract from the *Yorkshire Post*, 1967; pp. 158, Oxford University Press for extracts from S. Abbott, *The Prevention of Racial Discrimination in Britain*, 1971; p. 159, Routledge Publishers for an extract from J. Rex and S. Tomlinson, *Colonial Immigrants in a British City*, 1979.

Every effort has been made to contact the holders of copyright material. If any have been inadvertently overlooked, the publishers will be pleased to make the necessary arrangements at the first opportunity.

Contents

1 *Introduction*

To the reader

Look at these headlines, all of which were published in British newspapers during the last few years. They illustrate some of the major social and economic developments that have taken place in Britain in recent times. Can you identify which these developments are? How much do you know about them? Which other recent developments, not illustrated here, have had important effects on British society and the British economy?

Look at the headlines and make a list of the topics to which they relate (the top right headline, for example, relates to 'industrial developments'). Then add to your list any other topics that might help you understand British society and the British economy today.

UK 'years behind' in productivity

Hattersley says Labour will abolish the Lords

Privatization opposed

Infant deaths fall to their lowest level

Crisis over woman bishop

Results of GCSE hailed as success

EEC rules may force reduction in farming

When you have made your list, compare it with the chapter headings for this book. What similarities and what differences do you notice between the two?

One of the main purposes of this book is to help you make sense of all these features of British society and the British economy. You may feel that you already know a lot about education or transport in modern Britain. You probably do. You are unlikely, however, to *understand* why education is as it is today or how it has passed through many different stages before taking on its present form. Through the assignments that follow, the book tries to give you a better understanding of how the past has helped to shape the present. It shows you present events 'in context', i.e. as things that can only be understood in relation to what went before. This is in fact one of the most important aims of all GCSE history syllabuses: 'to promote the acquisition of knowledge and understanding of human activity in the past, *linking* it ... *with the present*'.

What this book aims to do

This book has been written mainly for students following GCSE courses in British social and economic history. Parts of the book are also useful for students following GCSE courses in 18th, 19th and 20th century British history, as well as for those studying Unit 1 of the Scottish Standard Grade course. The following 18 chapters cover the main topics offered in GCSE syllabuses in British social and economic history. All relate to the period 1700 to the present day.

Each chapter consists of an introduction to the main themes of the topic, two assignments (each based on a range of sources), and suggestions for further activities. Assignments may be used in three main ways:

- As exercises that help you to understand some of the key features of the topics you are studying.
- As opportunities to practise some of the important GCSE history skills, such as handling evidence.
- As coursework assignments that may be submitted to count towards your final GCSE history grade.

The further activities can be used in similar ways. Many of these contain suggestions for *investigative* work, i.e. for tasks where you have to do much of the planning and finding of resources for yourself. All tasks are also excellent preparation for the kinds of question you are likely to come across in the examinations at the end of your course.

Both assignments and further activities have been carefully planned to make sure that you are given opportunities to do work related to all the assessment objectives laid down for GCSE history, as well as to examine the full range of evidence on which knowledge in history is based. The next section of this introduction looks at these assessment objectives and at what they mean in practice for you.

Assessment objectives

An assessment objective is simply something that you are expected to know, understand or do. All GCSE history syllabuses have the same assessment objectives. These cover the following main areas:

- knowledge and understanding
- concepts
- empathy
- evidence

The rest of this section looks at what you are expected to do in each of these five areas.

Knowledge and understanding

Following a GCSE history syllabus involves *knowing* a great deal about the topics you are studying. In order to do well in your history course it is essential that you acquire this knowledge. GCSE history is different, however, from some of the examination courses that it replaced in that it does *not* require you to memorise vast amounts of precise factual information. Questions will allow you to use the knowledge you have rather than penalising you for the knowledge you do not have. As well as knowledge, it is important therefore to concentrate on developing your *understanding* of the topics that you are studying. This involves asking yourself all the time questions such as: 'do I know what this word means?', 'why did this event happen?', 'why is this important?'. In studying the transport revolution, for example, it is not sufficient to know how many railways were built, who built them, and when they were built. This information is important, but much more important is to understand why railways were built, how people felt about them, and why they had such a major impact on the British economy and on British society.

Concepts

All GCSE history syllabuses test your ability to 'make use of and understand the concepts of cause and consequence, continuity and change, similarity and difference'. These are important because they are the ways in which you should be organising your knowledge and understanding of the topics you are studying. Many of the questions in this book have been chosen to give you practice in the use of these concepts.

'*Cause*' and '*consequence*' are concerned with why events and developments took place (causes) and what effects they had (consequences). You will need to distinguish between short-term and long-term causes and between short-term and long-term consequences. You will also need to make judgments about which causes you feel to have been most important and which consequences you feel had the biggest impact.

'*Continuity*' and '*change*', like cause and consequence, are two sides of the same coin. 'Continuity' means the ways in which aspects of life remained the same, while 'change' is concerned with those aspects which did not remain the same. In the case of both continuity and change you will also be concerned with the reasons why some things changed and some things didn't, with the extent to which change took place, and with comparisons between the various changes that you have been studying.

'*Similarity*' and '*difference*' are perhaps the most obvious pair in these sets of concepts, but it is easy to forget that in studying history you should always be making *comparisons*. The sorts of question that you should keep on asking are: 'how did the suffragettes differ in their aims and their methods?', 'how did people react in different ways to the introduction of restrictions on the employment of children?', 'what similarities are there between the industrial revolution of the late 18th and early 19th centuries and the 'industrial revolution' that many people think is taking place in the late 20th century?'. By asking and trying to answer questions like these you will understand better both sets of developments that you are trying to compare – in the same way that going abroad usually helps people to understand more about their own society.

As well as the concepts discussed above, GCSE history aims to develop your understanding of more specific concepts such as *democracy*, *laissez-faire*, and *socialism*. Some of the questions in the assignments are designed to help you understand these concepts. Make sure you refer to a dictionary if you are ever in doubt as to the meaning of any of these important historical terms.

Empathy

'*Empathy*' means being able to put yourself in the position of other people. In the case of history it means looking at events and developments 'from the perspective of people in the past'. This of course is really part of *understanding* the past. In trying to understand it is essential that you attempt to make sense of the thoughts and feelings of the people involved. Many of the assignments in this book will encourage you to do this, through a study of the evidence that tells us what these motives, attitudes, thoughts and feelings actually were.

Evidence

When we study the past we refer to *sources*. From these sources we obtain *evidence*. It is only because of this evidence, left behind by the past, that we are able to know and understand what the past was like. There are many different types of evidence. There are also many different skills involved in using it. The assignments in this book introduce you to all the main types of evidence. They also give you practice in all the necessary skills.

It is important that you think hard about the sources that you will be studying. This involves more than just trying to make sense of a source and putting its meaning into your own words – though this is a very important first step. You also need to think about any possible *bias* in a source, i.e. the ways in which it might be giving a one-sided view of events. This might include 'reading between the lines', identifying the author's attitudes, noticing the things that are left unsaid as well as the things that are said. You will also be thinking about the value of sources as evidence, pointing out both their strengths and weaknesses. In addition you will need to compare and contrast sources with each other in various ways. There are many opportunities in this book to practise each of these skills. The more you practise them the easier they will become.

Assignments and how to tackle them

As well as testing all these assessment objectives, the assignments provide you with opportunities to tackle many different kinds of question. These include the main types of question usually found in GCSE history coursework and GCSE history examinations. Most assignments involve both a number of questions requiring fairly short answers and one or more questions which ask for a longer response, e.g. an essay.

In tackling questions bear in mind the following advice:

1. Read questions carefully, noting key words.
2. Read or look at sources carefully, checking your answers at all times against the evidence you have been given.
3. Draw up a plan before you begin to write (in longer answers).
4. Argue a case, showing how your points help to answer the question.

5 Stick to the question, excluding all material that is irrelevant to what you are asked to do.

6 Organise your answer, putting the points in a proper sequence and (in longer answers) making use of paragraphs.

7 Take care with presentation, writing legibly and neatly, and checking spelling and punctuation.

If you are following one of the further activities suggested at the end of each chapter you may also need to do quite a lot of research on your own: in libraries or looking at evidence in your local environment. This will involve careful planning. In the case of assignments such as these it will be important to follow the procedure set out below:

- Work out a list of questions that you are trying to answer.
- Identify the sources that will help you to answer these questions.
- Collect evidence from the sources.
- Plan the way in which you are going to write up your findings.

How your work will be marked

Your work on the assignments in this book will be marked on how far you have been able to show the understanding or skills that the questions are trying to test. For example, if the question is asking you to *explain* why some event happened you will be marked according to how well you have *explained*. You will not be marked on how well you have told the story of the event. For each question there will be a number of 'levels of response'. You will receive marks according to which level your answer has reached. The kinds of level of response that would be used in marking a question are shown in the example on the left.

Within each level the marks awarded will depend on how clearly and fully you answer and on the extent to which you argue a case, stick to the question, and illustrate your general points with specific examples.

Question: Why, during the 1930s, did some parts of Britain prosper while others suffered from an economic decline? (15 marks)

MARKING SCHEME

Target: Understanding of causes

Level 1 *Either:* Describes economic developments during the 1930s, explanations being implied rather than stated

Or: Makes vague and/or random points about reasons for either prosperity or decline (1 - 3 marks)

Level 2 Makes simple comparisons, with little supportive detail (4 - 7 marks)

Level 3 Sustained comparison between prosperity and decline, with clear focus on reasons throughout (8 - 11 marks)

Level 4 Sustained comparison, with clear focus on reasons, showing an awareness of both short-term and long-term causes (12 - 15 marks)

History is interesting!

The main purpose of this book is to try to arouse your interest in history. This is one of the aims of all GCSE history syllabuses: to 'stimulate interest in and enthusiasm for the study of the past'. If you work your way through a good number of the assignments and further activities that follow you will find yourself interviewing elderly people about their experiences when they were young, wandering around your local town looking at 19th century buildings, studying clips from 1930s films, arguing about how society treats women, handling old objects and studying the ways in which changes in communications are transforming our lives. British social and economic history is no longer just learning off by heart the terms of the Factory Act of 1833 or the dates of the new textile machines of the late 18th century (important though these still are).

You will have probably chosen to do history for GCSE. Once you get involved in the activities that follow, I hope that you will be glad that you made this choice!

2 *Population Changes*
Since 1700

Look at the illustrations of Leeds below. These should help you to understand the extent to which Britain has changed during the last 200 years. Such changes are typical of what has happened to many parts of Britain. Vast areas of the country that are now densely populated were at one time fields or open spaces. Parts of Britain which today are criss-crossed by motorways and covered with housing developments were inhabited not long ago by tiny numbers of people living in small villages and scattered settlements. Both the appearance of the country and the experiences of those living in it have changed almost beyond recognition.

There are many reasons why changes such as the ones illustrated in Sources A and B below took place. You will be considering some of these in later chapters of this book. Perhaps the main reason was that Britain's population grew more rapidly during this period than ever before: from approximately 7.5 million (for England, Wales and Scotland) in 1750 to almost 49 million 200 years later. As far as we know there had never, in the whole history of the world, been a population increase as rapid as this. It is often referred to as the 'demographic revolution' ('demographic' meaning to do with population). The first assignment (2.1) in this chapter is concerned with this demographic revolution and asks you to investigate both why it happened and the effects that it has had.

The population of Britain has not just grown — it has also come to be distributed in very different ways across the various parts of the country. In particular there has been a big shift from the countryside to the towns. In 1700 almost everyone lived in the countryside and worked on the land. Today most people live in towns or other urban settlements and have no direct contact with agriculture. These changes have taken place partly because of a great deal of migration (or movement of people) from one part of the British Isles to another. There has in addition been a large amount of emigration (movement of people *out* of the country) and immigration (movement of people *into* the country). The second assignment (2.2) in this chapter looks at emigration from Britain during the 19th century. Chapter 19 examines the experiences of some of the immigrants who came to this country from the late 19th century onwards.

Assignment 2.1
The population explosion

Source A
Total population of England and Wales (in thousands)

1700	5475	(estimate)
1720	5565	(estimate)
1740	6064	(estimate)
1760	6736	(estimate)
1780	7953	(estimate)
1801	8893	
1821	12 000	
1841	15 914	
1861	20 006	
1881	25 974	
1901	32 528	
1921	37 887	
1951	43 758	
1961	46 105	

Studying population changes involves making use of statistics. This assignment is designed to give you some practice in handling these statistics. Since 1801 a census of Britain's population has been taken every ten years (with the exception of 1941). This means that we have precise information about many aspects of population in each of those years: the numbers of males and females, the proportions of people in different age groups, and the distribution of the population in different parts of the country. Since 1838 (in England and Wales) and 1855 (in Scotland) all births, marriages and deaths have also had to be registered. This gives us further information about birth and death rates, about the average age at which people get married, etc.

With all this information we are able to understand a great deal about how population has changed in Britain over the last 200 years. It is not always quite so simple, however, to explain why some of these changes have come about. This assignment explores both the how and the why of population growth during the years since 1700.

Source B

Total number of baptisms (1700 – 1820) and total number of births per 1000 population (from 1840), England and Wales

Year	Baptisms (in thousands)
1700	157
1720	160
1740	174
1760	193
1780	228
1800	255
1820	344

Births per 1000 population (e.g. 32.2 in 1841 means that for every 1000 people in England and Wales there were on average 32.2 births in that particular year)

1841	32.2
1861	34.6
1881	33.9
1901	28.5
1921	22.4
1938	15.1

Source C

Total number of burials (1700 – 1820) and number of deaths per 1000 population (from 1840), England and Wales

Year	Burials (in thousands)
1700	137
1720	166
1740	173
1760	161
1780	198
1800	208
1820	208

Deaths per 1000 population (e.g. the figure 21.6 for 1841 means that for every 1000 people in England and Wales, there were on average 21.6 deaths in that year)

1841	21.6
1861	21.6
1881	18.9
1901	16.9
1921	12.1
1938	11.6

Source D

Population of some of the major towns of England and Wales (in thousands)

	1801	1821	1841	1861	1881	1901	1921
Birmingham	71	102	202	351	546	760	919
Bradford	13	26	67	106	183	280	286
Cardiff	2	4	10	33	83	164	200
Exeter	17	23	31	34	38	47	60
Leeds	53	84	152	207	309	429	458
Manchester	75	135	252	399	502	645	730
Oxford	12	16	24	28	35	49	57
Preston	12	25	51	83	97	113	117
Sunderland	24	31	43	78	117	146	159
Wigan	11	18	26	38	48	82	89

Activities

1 Turn the information in Source A into a graph. What do you notice about the changes that have taken place in the population of England and Wales during the years 1700 – 1961?

2 Do you think that the information contained in Source A is likely to be reliable? Explain your answer.

3 (i) Turn the information in Source B into two graphs (one for baptisms and the other for births per 1000 population). Then turn the information in Source C into two graphs (one for burials and the other for deaths per 1000 population).

(ii) What do you learn from these graphs about changes in (a) the birth rate and (b) the death rate during the period 1700 – 1938? Before answering this question, explain in your own words what is meant by 'birth rate' and 'death rate'.

4 Do your answers to Question 3 help you to explain the changes in the total population of England and Wales recorded in Source A?

5 What reasons help to explain the changes that have taken place in birth and death rates during this period?

6 Turn the information in Source D into a graph. What do you learn from this graph about the rates at which population increased in these towns? How might you explain the differences that you notice?

Assignment 2.2
Emigration from Britain in the 19th century

We tend to take it for granted that English is a world language. We know that in every continent there are large numbers of people who speak English as a first language. We also know that it is studied as a first foreign language in many other countries. The purpose of this assignment is to explore how and why this has come about. It looks at the main reason why the English language has spread: the emigration of large numbers of English-speaking people to many different parts of the world. This emigration continued throughout the 18th, 19th and 20th centuries. The assignment concentrates on emigration during the middle years of the 19th century. The main purpose is to find out why people emigrated and to learn something about the conditions that they experienced during the long journey to their new homes.

Source A
From *The Colonist*, 1848. This magazine was published by the Society for the Promotion of Colonisation, a group mainly interested in emigration to Australia.

You find trade bad; you are out of work; you scarcely make the two ends meet at the best of times; things do not look as if they would improve; they may grow worse; and you feel, do all you can, working early and late, that you and those you love best may sink from the station you hold and even starve at last.

Source B
From a pamphlet called '*America and England Contrasted: or, the 'Emigrants' Handbook and Guide to the United States'*, published in London in 1845

America is a country overflowing with prosperity and happiness – one which knows not the meaning of internal **tumult** – one in which all the citizens, with scarcely an exception, can command the necessities of life.

tumult: conflict/disorder

Source C

From a poem first published in a working man's magazine in 1844

The Emigrants' Farewell to England

Wretched poor! with all your sorrows,
Bless't with something called Poor Laws,
Oft were felt the keenest horrows
As were scann'd each hated clause,
But no more shall they offend us; –
Loud we'll sound their funeral **knell:**
Kinder **climes** *shall soon befriend us! –*
Land of Bastiles Fare thee well!

Ills so dire, and so distressing,
Bid us hasten from the spot,
Hoping soon't enjoy the blessing
Of a far more happy lot!
England! each of us have tried it,
And if there's another H-11,
Grant, kind Heaven! we may avoid it;–
Land of misery Fare thee well!

knell: the sounding of a bell
climes: climates

Source D

From a poem published in the same working man's magazine in 1844

Thoughts on Going to America

Elated with hope, I contemplate a land,
Which oppression has never subdued; –
A People who will not submit to the hand
Of a ruler despotic and rude.

....

There, there I still hope with the blessing of God!
To find an asylum of Peace; –
A happy retreat from grim tyranny's rod,
And from bondage a lasting release.

Source E

Numbers of emigrants from the United Kingdom, taken from the *Thirty-third General Report to the Emigration Commissioners, 1873*. The figures are in thousands and show the numbers of emigrants from the UK to different parts of the world.

Emigration from the United Kingdom in the years 1835–60

Year	British North America	United States	Australia and New Zealand	All other places	Totals for each year
1835	16	27	2	0.3	45
1836	34	38	3	0.3	75
1837	30	37	5	0.3	72
1838	5	14	14	0.3	33
1839	13	34	16	0.2	62
1840	32	41	16	2	91
1841	38	45	33	3	119
1842	54	64	9	2	128
1843	24	28	3	2	57
1844	23	44	2	2	71
1845	32	59	1	2	96
1846	43	82	2	2	130
1847	110	142	5	1	258
1848	31	188	24	5	248
1849	41	219	32	6	299
1850	33	233	16	9	281
1851	43	267	22	4	336
1852	33	244	88	4	369
1853	35	231	61	3	330
1854	44	193	83	3	323
1855	18	103	52	3	177
1856	16	112	45	4	177
1857	21	127	61	4	213
1858	10	60	39	5	114
1859	7	70	31	12	120
1860	10	87	24	7	128

Source F

The screw steamer, *City of Glasgow*, 1610 tons, at Philadelphia, USA. This ship was the first steamer regularly to carry steerage passengers to America. (Steerage passengers did not have cabins and sat on or beneath the decks.) It disappeared during a transatlantic crossing in 1854, with 430 people on board.

Source G

The Last of England, painted in 1852 by Ford Madox Brown. The painter was inspired to create this work by the experience of saying farewell to a friend who was leaving England on board an emigrant ship.

Source H

From a letter written aboard the ship *Washington* by an Irishman called Vere Foster, 1 December 1850. Vere Foster had travelled to America as a steerage passenger.

On the 30 th October no provisions had yet been served out, and the complaints of the poorer passengers in the steerage were naturally increasing, as they had no means of living, excepting on the charity of those who had brought extra provisions. At their request I drew up a letter, of which the following is a copy, addressed to the captain of the ship, A. Page:

Respected Sir,
We, the undersigned passengers on board the ship Washington, paid for and secured our passages in her in the confident expectation that the allowance of provisions promised in our contract tickets would be faithfully delivered to us. Four entire days having expired since the day on which ... the ship was appointed to sail, and three entire days since she actually sailed from the port of Liverpool, without our having received one particle of the stipulated provisions excepting water, and many of us having made no provision to meet such an emergency, we request that you will inform us when we may expect to commence receiving the allowance which is our due.

(signed)

Vere Foster
James Molony
John Collins
Jas. McNamara
John Hickey
Samuel Thorn
James Ward
Thomas Hotchin
Denis Mangan
Charles O'Donoghue
H. Hopkins

P.S. – From want of conveniences of writing, but particularly from the fear of being interfered with by the officers of the ship, no more signatures have been proceeded with, otherwise nearly 900 might have been added. While writing the former part of this letter at the request of my fellow passengers, the first mate, Mr. Williams, knocked me down flat upon the deck with a blow in the face.

Another day has elapsed without provisions being served out.
31 October 1850 (signed) Vere Foster.

.... On the morning of the 31st October, I presented the letter to Captian Page. He asked me the purport of it, and bade me read it. Having read out one-third of it, he said that was enough, and that he knew what I was; I was a damned pirate, a damned rascal, and that he would put me in irons and on bread and water throughout the rest of the voyage. The first mate then came up, and abused me foully and blasphemously and pushed me down, bidding me get out of that, as I was a damned b ------.

... The first and second mates, the surgeon and the man specially appointed to look after the passengers, and the cooks – all these very seldom open their lips without prefacing what they have to say, with "God damn your soul to hell, you damned b------", or "by Jesus Christ I'll rope end's you", or some other expression from the same category ...

25 th November – Another child, making about 12 in all, died of dysentery from want of proper nourishing food, and was thrown into the sea sown up, along with a great stone, in a cloth.

Activities

1 Study Sources A, B, C and D. Explain in your own words the reasons for emigration suggested in each of these sources.

2 How reliable are Sources A, B, C and D as evidence for the reasons why people emigrated?

3 (i) Before making use of Source E, what questions would you want to ask in order to check its accuracy?

(ii) Assuming that the information in Source E is accurate, what do you learn from this source about emigration and the possible causes of emigration?

4 Study Sources F, G and H. What do you learn from these sources about the ways in which emigrants travelled to their new homes?

5 Ford Madox Brown (Source G) was trying to create a work of art; Vere Foster (Source H) was trying to persuade the government to do something to improve conditions on board emigrant ships. Does this mean that both sources are unreliable? Explain your answer.

Further activities

1 Study the changes in population that have taken place in your own area since the beginning of the 18th century (if figures are available) or since the first census in 1801.
(i) How does the growth of population in your area compare with the rate of growth in Britain's population as a whole?
(ii) Give reasons for the changes that you have identified and comment on the effects that they have had.

2 Study the census enumerators' returns for your own area for one of the 19th century censuses. You may obtain this information on a computer database (if available), on a photocopy of the original return, or on a transcription (copy) of the return.

(i) Familiarise yourself with the information contained in these returns and then decide on *three* questions (of interest to a historian) that you think might be answered by studying them in detail. Examples of questions include the following: What proportion of women worked as domestic servants? What was the average family size? What proportion of the population was born locally? What proportion of adult males worked in industry/on the land?

(ii) Having asked your three questions, try to answer them using the evidence available in the census. What do your answers to these questions tell you about 19th century life?

3 (For those of you who have access to the relevant information.)
(i) Draw a family tree for your own family, tracing it as far back into the 19th century as possible. Write brief biographical notes about the various people on this family tree.

(ii) What do you learn from this exercise about (a) family size, (b) migration (whether into, out of or within the United Kingdom), and (c) age at death? In each case try to give reasons for any changes or patterns that you notice.

3 *Agriculture*
1750 – 1870

During the 18th and early 19th centuries most people in Britain lived in the countryside. Most of them also worked on the land. In order to understand British society during these years it is essential therefore to study the major developments that affected agriculture.

Although it is probably misleading to talk about an 'agricultural revolution', there is no doubt that the period 1750–1870 was one of rapid agricultural change. There is also no doubt that these changes had far-reaching effects on the people who lived and worked on the land. Once you begin to study this topic in detail, however, you will soon realise that the pace of change varied enormously from one part of the country to another. Some areas were already enclosed at the beginning of the 18th century; others were still unenclosed in 1850. In some places enclosure led to an increase in the amount of arable farming; in others it led to a decrease. Some farmers were quick to take up new developments such as crop rotation amd scientific stock breeding; others stuck to their old methods with hardly any change. Some made increasing use of new machines; others carried on as if they had not been invented.

The first asssignment (3.1) in this chapter looks at the effects of enclosure in one particular area. In working on this assignment, don't assume therefore that what happened in that area was necessarily typical of the country as a whole. The second assignment (3.2) also focuses on an aspect of change: the growing use of mechanical inventions. Don't assume, again, that all farmers adopted these machines as soon as they were invented. Many continued to sow, reap and thresh in ways that had changed little over the centuries.

One reason why this topic is important is because it helps you understand how our present landscape came about. Look at the aerial photograph (Source D) on p. 17. This is a landscape that is familiar to people in most parts of the country. We tend to assume that the countryside has always looked like this. In fact it has only done so for the last 200 years as a result of human activity in the 18th and 19th centuries. If you study closely the kind of landscape that you find in Source D, you will find that roads, hedges, ditches and fields all have their origins at that time. Even trees that you see today may well have been planted at the time when the land was first enclosed. It is important to try to follow up the assignments in this chapter with a study of the landscape in your own local area (if this is possible). The further activities section at the end of the chapter contains some suggestions as to how you might set about doing this.

Assignment 3.1
The effects of enclosure

The sources in this assignment all relate to Northamptonshire and are mostly concerned with enclosure in that county in the late 18th and early 19th centuries. Northamptonshire was a county that experienced a great deal of enclosure at that time. The purpose of the assignment is to look at what was involved in enclosure and to assess some of its effects.

Source A
A map showing the village of Geddington, c. 1717

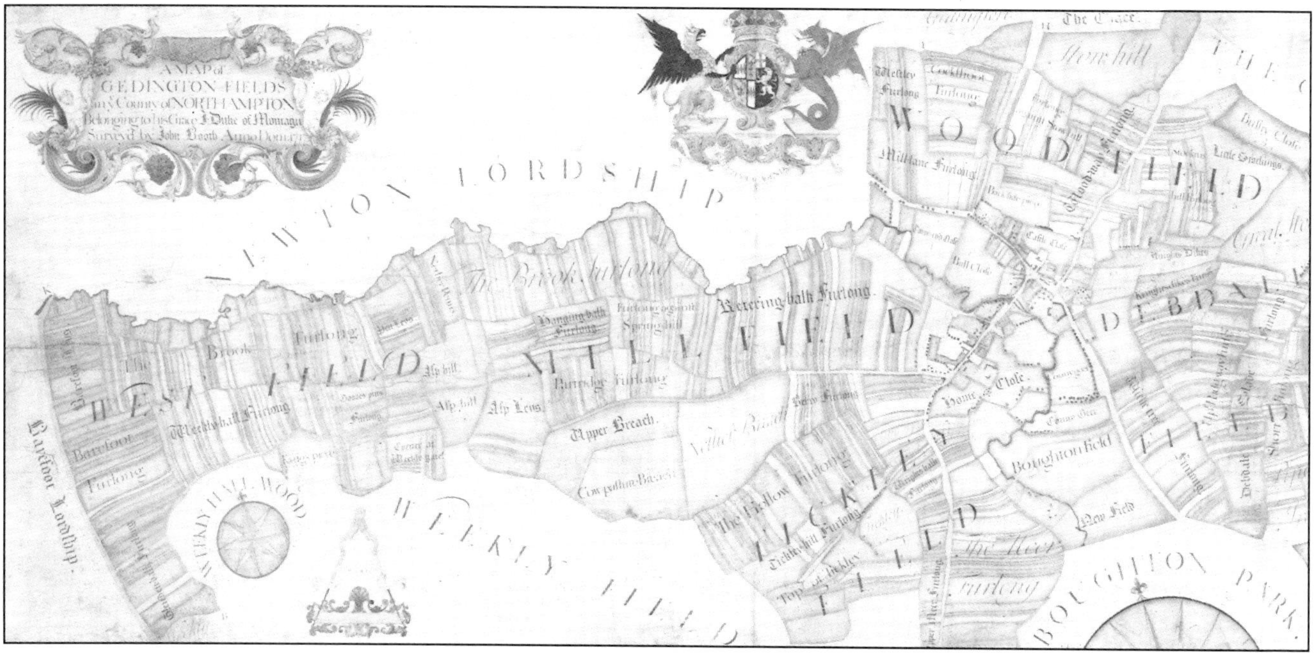

Source B A map of the village of Helpston, c. 1779

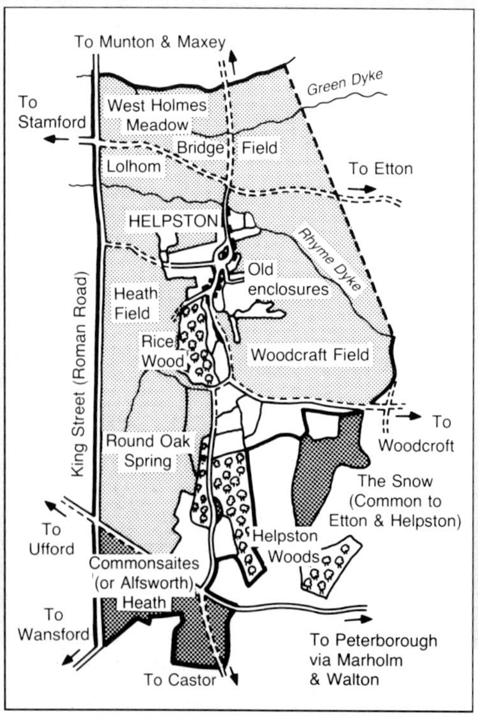

Source C A map of the village of Helpston, c. 1827. The Enclosure Act for Helpston was passed in 1809.

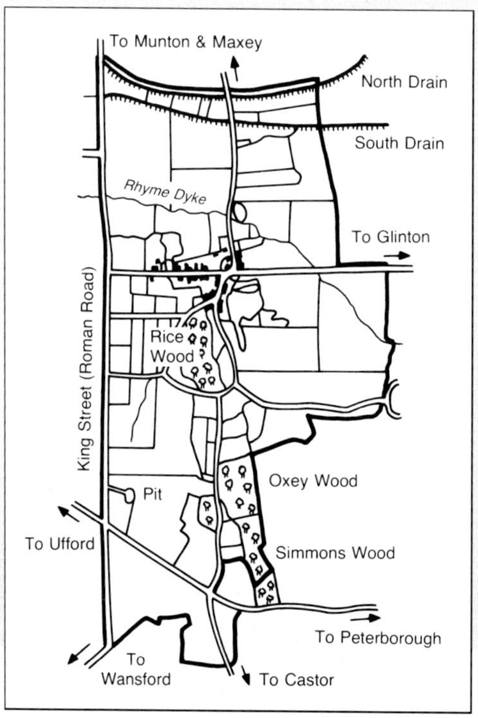

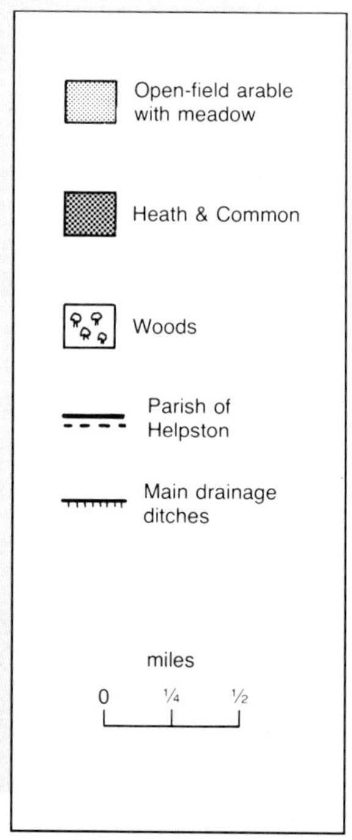

Source D
An aerial photograph of Braunston. The Enclosure Act for this area was passed in 1775.

Source E

William Pitt, *General View of Northamptonshire*, 1809

Kettering Common Field, lately enclosed, about two thousand acres; rent, when open £1 to £1 10s per acre, but since enclosed, worth from £2 to £3 15s per acre; but some of the richest land near the town thrown to grass, or intended for it, the breadth of corn grown here will in consequence be lessened, but the quantity grown per acre doubtless increased.

Source F

W.G. Hoskins, *The Making of the English Landscape*, 1955

A great number of new by-roads came into existence as a result of the enclosure movement. They are immediately recognisable on the one-inch map by the manner in which they run from village to village practically straight across country, with perhaps an occasional sudden right-angled bend and then on again. More significantly still, these straight roads sometimes do not run to the nearest village but continue for some miles through open country, reaching the villages by means of side-roads. There is none of that apparently aimless wandering in short stretches, punctuated by frequent bends, going halfway round the compass to reach the next hamlet or village, which characterises the by-roads in country that has never been in open field or left it several centuries ago. On the six-inch and twenty-five inch maps, too, the parliamentary enclosure roads stand out conspicuously with their wide grass verges. The road runs like a grey ribbon between verges full of tall grasses, cow-parsley, and dog-roses ...

Source G

Extracts from the poems of John Clare, a famous early 19th century poet. Clare was born in 1793 in Helpston, Northamptonshire. As a boy of seven he was set to watch sheep and geese on the common heathland. He knew Helpston both before and after enclosure and had strong views about the changes that he saw taking place.

(1) Dire nakedness o'er all prevails;
Yon fallows bare and brown
Are all beset with posts and rails
And turned upside down.

(2) Fence meeting fence in owner's little bounds
Of field and meadow, large as garden-grounds,
In little parcels little minds to please,
With men and flocks imprisoned, ill at ease.

(3) ***Ye*** *injur'd fields, ye once were gay,*
When Nature's hand displayed
Long waving rows of willows grey
And clumps of hawthorn shade;
But now, alas! your hawthorn bowers
All desolate we see!
The spoiler's axe their shade devours,
And cuts down every tree.
Not trees alone have owned their force,
Whole woods beneath them bowed,
They turned the winding ***rivulet's*** *course,*
And all thy pastures plough'd.

(4) Ye fields, ye scenes so dear ...
Ye meadow-blooms, ye pasture-flowers, farewell!
Ye banish'd trees, ye make me deeply sigh -
Inclosure came, and all your glories fell:

Ye: you
rivulet: stream

Activities

1 Study Sources A and B.

(i) In what ways was the landscape of Helpston in 1779 similar to that of Geddington in 1717?

(ii) What do you learn from these sources about the methods of farming used in these two villages?

2 Study Sources B and C.

(i) List all the changes that had taken place in Helpston between 1779 and 1827.

(ii) Explain in each case why these changes had been made.

3 (i) What do you learn from Source D about farming methods (a) before enclosure and (b) after enclosure?

(ii) How valuable are aerial photographs as evidence for agricultural changes in the 18th and 19th centuries?

4 In what ways does Source F help you to understand Sources C and D? Refer to the sources in support of your answer.

5 (i) Identify the two effects of enclosure mentioned in Source E.
(ii) Why do you think enclosure had these effects?

6 Study Source G carefully . You may not be used to reading poems of this kind. They are actually much easier than they seem at a glance.

(i) Make a list of the things that Clare dislikes about the changes that have taken place in his village. Don't miss the less obvious points, e.g. in the first poem as well as complaining about all the fences he seems to be objecting to the way in which pasture land has been ploughed and to the fact that everything has been 'turned upside down'.

(ii) Are the changes mentioned by Clare the same as those that you have identified in your answer to 2 (i)? Refer in detail to the sources in support of your answer.

(iii) Is Clare a useful source? Explain your answer.

(iv) As a member of a poor farming family, what other criticisms of enclosure might Clare have made?

Assignment 3.2
Farming implements and machines

Unlike the industrial revolution, new machines played only a small part in the agricultural changes of the 18th century. Most farmers were still sowing seed by hand as late as the mid-19th century, over 100 years after Jethro Tull had first tried to promote the use of the seed-drill. Threshing machines (1780s onwards) and reaping machines (1820s onwards) were also slow to be adopted. Perhaps the period of greatest change was the mid-19th century, during the so-called 'golden years' of British farming, when many machines came into more widespread use. This assignment looks at some of these machines and also at the farming methods they were designed to replace.

Source A

A 19th century print showing the reaping machine invented by Patrick Bell in 1826. Reaping machines were not widely used before the 1850s.

Source B

A winnowing machine from a catalogue issued in 1772. The grain and chaff were tipped into the hopper at the top. Fans turned by hand blew out the chaff while the grain fell down at one side.

Source C
A common drill sowing machine – an illustration from J. Slight and R. Scott Burn, *The Book of Farm Implements and Machines,* 1858

Source D
A threshing machine, from Copland's *Agriculture Ancient and Modern,* 1866

Activities

1 (i) Describe briefly in your own words the purpose of each of these machines.

(ii) Place the four machines in the order in which they would have been used in the course of the farming year.

(iii) What traditional methods of farming were these machines intended to replace? Describe each of these traditional methods, using labelled illustrations where appropriate.

2 Study Source A.

(i) Describe how this machine works.

(ii) What do you think might have been the advantages of this machine when compared with traditional methods of reaping?

(iii) Why, despite these possible advantages, was this machine so slow to be adopted?

3 Study Source B. Does this machine have any advantages by comparison with traditional methods of winnowing? Explain your answer.

4 Study Source C.

(i) Copy this drawing and label the various parts in order to show how it worked.

(ii) What were the advantages of this machine by comparison with hand sowing?

(iii) Why, despite these advantages, was hand sowing still widely practised in the mid-19th century?

5 Study Source D.

(i) Describe what is happening in this scene.

(ii) How is the source of power for this machine different from that used by the machines in Sources A, B and C?

(iii) In what ways and to what extent did this machine (a) reduce costs and (b) increase costs? Refer in detail to the source in support of your answer.

6 Is it possible to single out one of the following factors as the one that had the greatest influence on the development of farming during the years 1850 – 70?

- the introduction of machinery
- growth in population
- improved transport
- the effects of enclosure

Explain your answer.

Further activities

1 Investigate enclosure and its effects within your own local area. Write up your report under the following headings:

- when and how (e.g. by Act of Parliament) enclosure took place
- changes in field patterns
- effects on common land
- new roads
- drainage
- hedges and trees
- gains and losses for particular social groups

Evidence that will be useful includes: Ordnance Survey maps (especially 25-inch); enclosure and/or estate plans: the evidence on the ground; any relevant written sources.

2 If you live in or near a rural area (or an area that was rural in the 18th and 19th centuries) study the buildings that date from the period 1750–1870. What do you learn from these buildings about (a) the architecture, (b) the society (e.g. the existence of different social classes), and (c) the way of life of your area during that period?

3 Why was there so much interest in agricultural improvement during the 18th and early 19th centuries? In the course of your answer, try to arrange possible reasons in what you think might be their order of importance.

4 Compare farming in your part of Britain today with farming in the first half of the 19th century. What similarities and differences do you notice between the two periods?

4 *Agriculture*
from the Mid-19th Century to the Present Day

Since the development of farming in prehistoric times most people in the British Isles had been engaged in agriculture. They worked on the land and lived in small rural communities. The industrial revolution of the 18th and 19th centuries changed all this. By the mid-19th century a major shift from agriculture to industry and from countryside to towns had taken place. The 1851 census showed clearly that most people no longer worked on the land or lived in the countryside. Since that time the trend has intensified. At the end of the 20th century the overwhelming majority of the population live in urban areas and agricultural workers form only a tiny proportion of the total workforce. The story of agriculture since 1850 is therefore partly a story of decline. It is also, however, a story of survival and of adaptation to changed conditions.

The period begins in the mid-19th century when agricultural prosperity was at its peak. The growth in population had led to increasing demand for agricultural produce. New lands were being cultivated and new methods introduced. Rents, profits and wages had never been so high.

This 'golden age' of 'high farming' did not, however, last. From the late 1870s onwards Britain was flooded with cheap foreign grain and meat – from North America, Australia, New Zealand and Argentina. Improved steamships and the opening up of the prairies by railway meant that vast quantities of agricultural goods could be sold on the British market at prices much lower than anything produced at home. As a free trade country, Britain placed no restrictions on any of these imports. The effect on British agriculture was the 'great agricultural depression' of the last quarter of the 19th century. It is this depression that you will be studying in the first of the two assignments in this chapter (4.1). As Assignment 4.1 will show you, this depression had varying effects in different parts of the country. Some farmers were better able to survive than others. Many were forced to adapt to new conditions, concentrating on produce that was less likely to suffer from foreign competition, such as dairy farming and fruit growing.

This story of survival has continued throughout the 20th century. British farmers have learnt to farm more economically and scientifically, making use of more machines and fewer labourers. By the late 20th century British farming had become one of the most intensive in the world. The story of 20th century agriculture is not, however, just a simple success story. Many farmers struggled and failed – especially in the inter-war years. New methods have also had some very damaging effects on the environment of our overcrowded island.

Assignment 4.2 examines the development of British agriculture in the inter-war period. It is intended to give you practice in handling historical statistics. The further activities section at the end of the chapter suggests ways in which you might investigate more recent developments, in particular the very important effect on agriculture of Britain's entry into the European Community.

Assignment 4.1
The 'Great Depression' of British agriculture, 1873 – 96

The words 'Great Depression' in the title have deliberately been put in inverted commas. This is to show that some historians feel it is misleading to describe as a 'depression' the changes that took place in British agriculture at the end of the 19th century. These people agree that major changes took place in agriculture during this period. They disagree, however, with those who see the last quarter of the 19th century as simply a period of decay. The purpose of this assignment is to help you make up your own mind about the extent to which British agriculture was affected by this 'depression'. It is also intended to give you practice in using historical statistics.

SOURCE A
From the *Final Report of the Royal Commission on Agriculture,* 1897

... With a few exceptions **the seasons** since 1882 have been on the whole satisfactory from the agricultural point of view; and the evidence before us has shown that the existing depression, as we have already stated in our Second Report, is to be attributed mainly to the fall in prices of farm produce.

... while there has been a general downward tendency in (the) prices (of agricultural products), the fall has been most marked in the case of grain, particularly wheat; and wool also has fallen heavily. Under these circumstances, we are not surprised to find that the facts at our disposal indicate that the depression is much more acute in the arable counties (particularly in those districts where the climate is not favourable for laying down permanent or temporary pastures) than elsewhere ... in counties where the surroundings are such as to favour dairying, market-gardening, poultry farming and other special industries, the conditions are somewhat more favourable. While it is true, however, that the effects of the depression are less **manifest** in some districts than in others, we are unable to point to any part of the country in which they can be said to be entirely absent ...

The arable section of England ... includes ... the counties of Bedford, Berks., Buckingham, Cambridge, Essex, Hants., Hertford, Huntingdon, Kent, Leicester, Lincoln, London, Middlesex, Norfolk, Northampton, Notts., Oxford, Rutland, Suffolk, Surrey, Sussex, Warwick, and York (East Riding) ...

The grass section ... includes ... the counties of Chester, Cornwall, Cumberland, Derby, Devon, Dorset, Durham, Gloucester, Hereford, Lancashire, Monmouth, Northumberland, **Salop**, Somerset, Stafford, Westmoreland, Wilts., Worcester, York (North Riding), and York (West Riding ...

Arable section of England ...

Among the counties included in this section, Essex appears, from the evidence we have received, to have suffered more severely than any other. Mr Hunter Pringle, who reported upon the Ongar, Chelmsford, Maldon, and Braintree districts of the county, states, "The depression of agriculture in Essex appears to have commenced about 1875, when the price of wheat fell from, say, 55s to 45s per quarter ... Between 1875 and 1879 many farmers failed or gave up, but new tenants were easily found at slightly reduced rents ... The consequences of 1879 were to severely cripple the old tenants, to ruin many of the new ones, and to inflict heavy losses upon landlords farming their own

Source A continued on next page ...

Source A continued...

property. Between 1880 and 1884 the number of farms given up either in despair or for reasons over which the occupiers had no control was stated to have been enormous ... A regular panic set in; some tenants who had hitherto weathered the storm refused to renew their leases upon any terms, while others continued from year to year at large reductions. From figures given to me in Essex it will be seen ... that rents were reduced between 1880 and 1886 from 25 to as much as 80 per cent ... Only those who kept a considerable head of stock, or took to cow-keeping, appear to have withstood the consequences of bad seasons or low prices, and still continue in occupation ..."

Grazing section of England

The evidence relating to the counties of Salop, Herefordshire, Monmouthshire and Worcestershire indicates that the effects of depression here have not been so manifest as in other parts of the country, except in arable districts with strong soils. Dairying and grazing are the chief branches of farming in these counties. In Herefordshire and Worcestershire fruit and hops are largely grown, and in some parts of the latter county, market gardening is carried on with success. There are few farms unlet; on good grass lands, hop land, and dairy farms, rents have in many instances been maintained, and reductions have apparently seldom exceeded 15 per cent. On heavy soils and arable farms in Salop, Herefordshire and Worcestershire the reductions of rent have ranged from 20 to 30 per cent; in the Bridgnorth district up to 40 per cent .

the seasons: the weather
manifest: noticeable
Salop: Shropshire

	1867–9	1870–6	1894–1903
Wheat	35.38	27.56	7.72
Barley	16.78	17.56	9.43
Oats	10.54	9.07	8.07
Potatoes	14.02	13.82	11.34
Hay, straw, fruit and vegetables	20.11	19.40	21.75
Other crops	7.34	7.58	3.64
ARABLE	**104.17**	**94.99**	**61.95**
Beef	34.90	45.67	42.05
Mutton	25.92	30.51	25.20
Pig meat	18.60	22.95	19.13
Horses	1.50	2.00	3.00
Milk	33.78	38.51	43.56
Wool	7.49	8.27	3.24
Poultry and eggs	4.57	6.96	10.00
LIVESTOCK	**126.76**	**154.87**	**146.18**
TOTAL	**230.93**	**249.86**	**208.13**
Index	100	108	90

Source B

Output of UK agriculture (in millions of pounds)

Activities

1 Trace a map of England showing the counties as they were before the 1970s. On this map shade the arable and grazing sections of the country as listed in Source A. What do you notice about the distribution of these sections on your map?

2 Study Source A.

(i) What do you learn from Source A about the effects of the 'depression' in arable areas?

(ii) Why did the 'depression' have its strongest effects in arable areas?

(iii) Referring both to Source A and to your background knowledge, explain why some parts of England were less severely affected by the 'depression'.

3 In what ways does Source B support Source A?

Source C

A country labourer and his family, from *Our Village* by Mary Russell Mitford, 1879

4 What do you learn from Source B that you have not already learnt from Source A?

5 Study Source C, published at the height of the 'depression'. Does this source have any value to someone studying agriculture in late 19th century England?

6 Study Sources D and E.

(i) Describe in words what you learn from each of the maps in Source D about agricultural change in the Chilterns.

(ii) Does Source D help to explain any of the changes that you have noticed in Source E? Give reasons for your answer.

7 Do changes in the Chilterns fit into the national pattern illustrated in Sources A and B? Explain your answer.

Source D

A map of the Chilterns

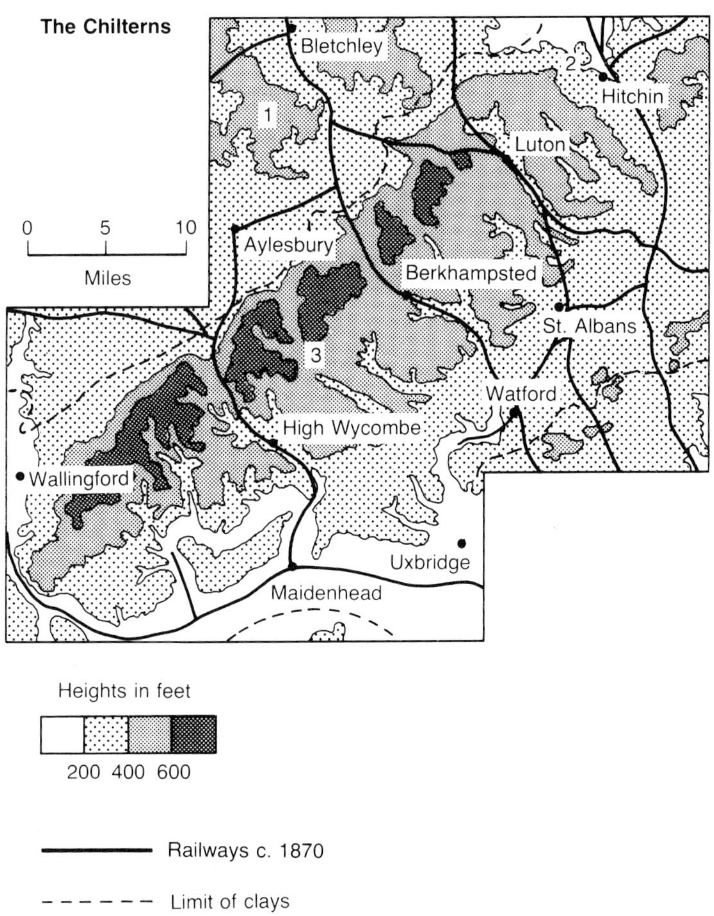

Source E

Maps showing changes in agriculture in the Chilterns, 1875 – 1900. The area covered by these maps is shown in Source C

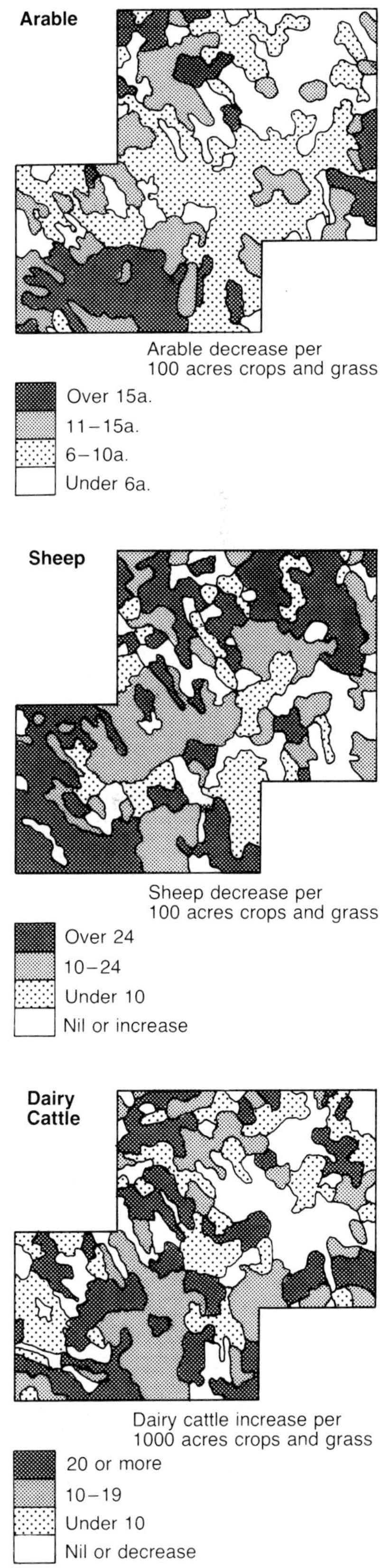

Assignment 4.2
Change and continuity in British agriculture during the inter-war years

During the 20th century many changes have taken place in British agriculture. Farming has become more mechanised and more scientific. It has also become less labour intensive, i.e. more is now produced with a smaller workforce. Governments have come to be involved in ways that would have been unthinkable in the 19th century: through the payment of subsidies, through assistance with marketing, and through a whole variety of controls. By increasing demand for agricultural goods, the two world wars and especially the Second World War (1939 – 45) greatly stimulated all these trends. More recently, Britain's membership of the European Community has led to even closer government regulation through the Community's Common Agricultural Policy.

This assignment is designed to help you study some of these changes. It also involves identifying ways in which agriculture did not change – or at least changed only slowly. The period to which the sources refer is that of the inter-war years. This was a period in which farmers experienced many problems. It was also one in which the foundations were laid for the later, more dramatic, changes of the 1940s onwards.

Source A
Cropping and livestock in England and Wales, 1910 – 39

	1910–14	1915–19	1920–24	1925–9	1930–34	1935–9
Cropping (thousand acres)						
Crops and grass	27 192	26 989	26 099	25 593	25 204	24 791
Permanent grass	15 990	15 395	14 688	15 274	15 748	15 720
Arable	11 202	11 594	11 411	10 319	9456	9071
Wheat	1794	2156	1821	1491	1450	1744
Barley	1496	1407	1416	1164	924	846
Oats	2017	2355	2120	1820	1582	1344
Potatoes	440	502	517	503	477	461
Turnips, swedes, and mangolds	1530	1343	1276	1062	844	667
Rotation grass	2587	2408	2542	2512	2351	2160
Livestock						
Cattle (thousands)	5844	5180	5701	6135	6311	6637
Sheep (thousands)	18 346	16 849	13 866	16 482	17 435	17 243
Pigs (thousands)	2390	2000	2528	2575	2933	3666
Fowls (millions)	–	–	30.8*	38.5	56.1	54.8

* 1924 only

Source B Output of UK agriculture, 1927–39

	£ million						
	1927-8	1933-4	1934-5	1935-6	1936-7	1937-8	1938-9
Livestock and wool*	78.1	62.5	63.8	65.1	71.1	73.6	68.8
Milk and products	55.0	52.1	52.9	54.1	55.8	59.3	64.6
Poultry and eggs	15.9	22.1	21.9	22.6	21.1	22.2	21.1
Grain crops*	22.6	9.2	10.1	10.0	12.4	12.4	10.0
Potatoes and sugar beet	17.1	14.2	18.8	19.5	20.4	16.6	15.8
Other crops	31.9	39.7	38.9	34.9	39.5	40.1	39.1
Total £	220.6	199.8	206.4	206.2	220.3	224.2	219.4

Source C Sugar beet in the UK, 1924–30

	No. of growers	Thousands of acres	Thousands of tons of beet	Thousands of tons refined sugar
1924-5	4,039	22.6	183.7	23.9
1925-6	10,504	56.2	431.2	51.7
1926-7	20,661	129.5	1117.1	153.3
1927-8	31,859	232.9	1,503.0	189.1
1928-9	25,050	178.0	1,369.8	193.6
1929-30	32,204	230.5	2,003.6	288.3

Source D Farmers declared bancrupt in England and Wales, 1927–39

Year	Average no.	Year	Average no.	Year	Average no.
1911-13	322	1924	360	1931	497
1914-16	133	1925	368	1932	600
1917-19	43	1926	342	1933	428
1920	44	1927	478	1934	288
1921	285	1928	462	1935	224
1922	403	1929	462	1936	215

Source E Agricultural workers in England and Wales, 1927 – 39

	Regular workers (thousands)				Casual workers (thousands)
Year	Males 21 yrs +	Males under 21 yrs	Females	Total	
1927	453	134	63	650	114
1929	452	125	67	644	126
1931	435	117	64	616	100
1933	423	114	60	597	120
1935	413	105	50	568	105
1937	395	95	46	536	96
1939	375	96	40	511	96

Source F

From W. B. Mercer, *Survey of the Agriculture of Cheshire*, 1963, referring to the 1930s

Sometimes a whole block of land passes out of cultivation in a matter of a few years and nothing remains except the names of the farmhouses and a few converted and modernised cottages. More commonly the absorption of agricultural lands is partial and chunks of land are cut off at irregular intervals ... Occasionally the tide of invasion seems to flow round farms leaving them substantially unaltered, or consisting of blocks of land behind housing frontages or of fields scattered among houses.

Activities

1 In the case of *each* of Sources A to F, try to answer the following three questions:

(i) What major changes in British agriculture are illustrated by this source?

(ii) How would you explain the changes that you have identified?

(iii) In what ways, if any, does this source suggest that agriculture did *not* change?

2 Use your answers to Question 1 to help you plan and write an answer to this question:

'During the 1920s and 1930s British agriculture continued to decline.'

Do you agree with this statement? Give reasons for your answer.

3 'Historical statistics are bound to be useful because they contain precise facts and figures.' Say whether or not you agree, supporting your answer by reference to Sources A to E.

Further activities

1 Study any Ordnance Survey maps of your local area that are available for the period since the mid-19th century. What changes do you notice in (a) the amount of land used for agricultural purposes, (b) field sizes, and (c) farm buildings? How would you explain the changes that you have identified?

2 If you live in or near an agricultural area, interview two people who worked in agriculture earlier in the 20th century. Plan your interviews so that you try to find out about (a) farming methods and (b) the lives of agricultural workers. Write up your accounts of the interviews, describing what you have learned and relating this to your own background knowledge.

3 How has British agriculture changed as a result of Britain's membership of the European Community? What arguments have been used to suggest that membership of the community has been (a) beneficial and (b) harmful?

5 *The Industrial Revolution*
1750–1870

When we think of the industrial revolution, scenes like the one in this photograph are often the first that spring to mind. Look closely at the photograph. Before reading on, try to identify the aspects of the industrial revolution that it illustrates...

You should have come up with some of the following:

- the building of large factories, in which production is mechanised
- the siting of factories in river valleys, in order to make use of water power
- the later introduction of steam power (hence factory chimneys)
- urbanisation and dense urban housing
- the building of railways
- a movement that was not closely regulated by government (look at the lack of any obvious planning in the development of housing)

There are further points that you might have made, such as pollution and the change in the environment.

All these, along with rapid economic growth (which is illustrated indirectly in the photograph), were important features of the industrial revolution. It would be misleading, however, to see the scene in the photograph as *typical* of the effects of the industrial revolution on different parts of Britain. The industrial revolution affected most industries, but it affected them in different ways. Photographs of Sheffield (iron and steel) and Stoke-on-Trent (pottery) would *not* look the same as this photograph of Saltaire (salt mills). The industrial revolution also had many indirect consequences, for example the impact on agriculture of better transport. The way of life of many rural districts changed dramatically as a result of the industrial revolution. At a glance, however, this might have been much less obvious.

This chapter concentrates on two of the most important features of industrialisation: the mechanisation of textile production and the growing use of iron. The assignments encourage you to ask three main questions about the industrial changes of the late 18th and early 19th centuries: Why did they take place? What did they involve? What effect did they have? The further activities section at the end of the chapter suggests ways of investigating the particular changes that took place in your own local area.

Assignment 5.1
New technology and the textile revolution

In the late 20th century we are still experiencing the industrial revolution that began in the 18th century. An important part of this revolution, then as now, has been the impact of new technology. In the 18th century it was spinning machines and steam engines. In the late 20th century it is microchips, robots and electronic mail. The technologies are very different, but the impact can be surprisingly similar.

This assignment looks at the effects of new technology on the cotton textile industry, Britain's most rapidly developing industry in the early part of the industrial revolution. It encourages you to investigate the nature of the new technology, to consider the impact it had, and to assess its importance as a cause of the industrial revolution.

Source A

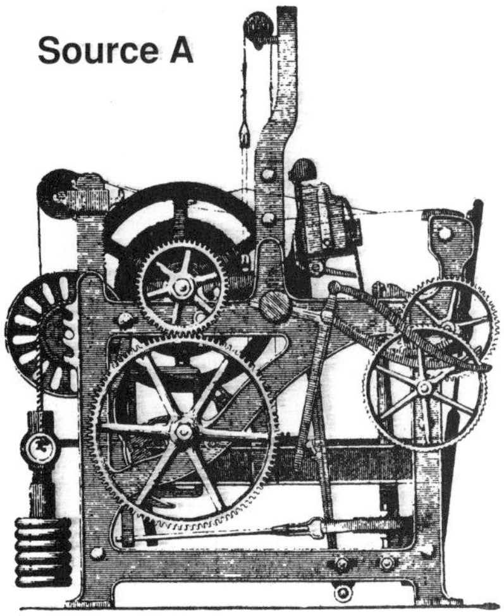

Source B

Source C

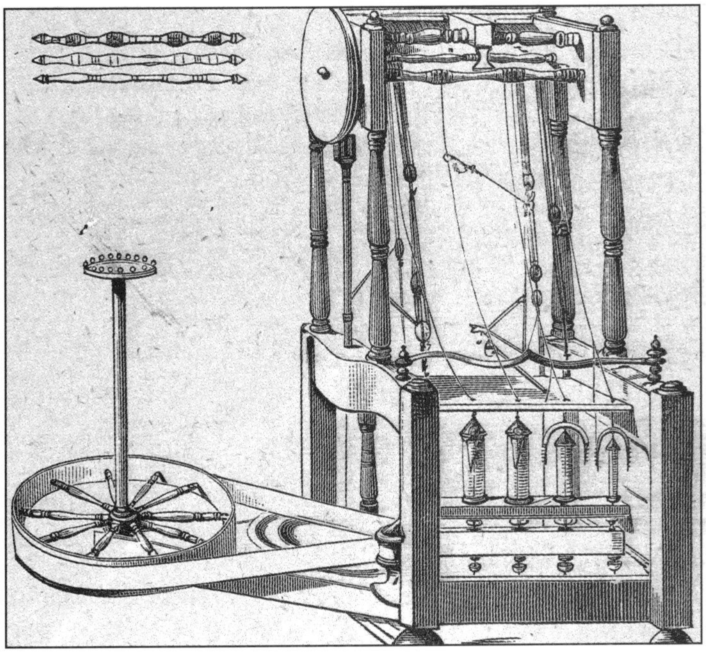

Source D

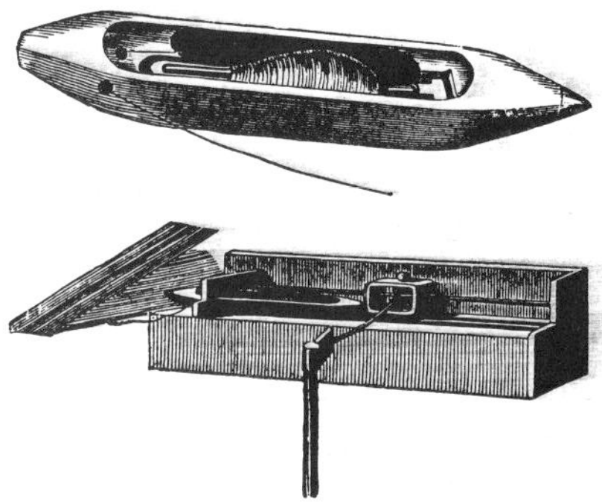

Source E

Source F

Activities

1 (i) Referring to accounts of textile inventions in your textbook, match Sources A to F against the following list of machines:

- Kay's flying shuttle
- Hargreaves' spinning jenny
- Arkwright's water frame
- Arkwright's carding machine
- Crompton's spinning mule
- Cartwright's power loom

(ii) In the case of each machine, explain why you made that particular identification.

(iii) Now arrange the machines in the order in which they were invented.

2 In the case of *two* of the machines that are illustrated:

(i) Describe in detail how the machine works. If this is helpful, illustrate your answer with a labelled diagram.

(ii) Explain why the machine was important in the development of the textile industry.

3 Was the invention of new textile machines the main cause of the industrial revolution of the late 18th and early 19th centuries? (As well as writing about new technology, you should consider the part played by other causes, e.g. the effects of the agricultural 'revolution', the growth of trade and its effects, the impact of the Revolutionary and Napoleonic Wars, the rapid rise in population.)

Assignment 5.2
The uses of iron

During the 18th and early 19th centuries major changes took place in the manufacture of iron goods. The most important of these were:

- the use of coke (instead of charcoal) for smelting, pioneered at the beginning of the 18th century by Abraham Darby
- Henry Cort's 'puddling and rolling' process which improved the strength and quality of 'wrought' iron
- James Neilson's 'hot blast' method, which greatly reduced the consumption of fuel
- the growing use of the steam engine

As with cotton textiles, iron production became increasingly mechanised, took place on a bigger and bigger scale, and adopted methods of mass production. As a result, as you can see from Source A, production increased very rapidly. This assignment looks at the reasons behind this increase. It also looks at the many uses to which all this iron was put.

Source A
Estimated annual production of iron

Year	Production (tonnes)
1750–54	26 000 (average per annum)
1770–74	40 000 (average per annum)
1780–84	62 000 (average per annum)
1800	180 000
1810	400 000
1820	320 000
1830	680 000
1840	1 400 000
1850	2 250 000

Source B
Hebden Bridge, Yorkshire, showing textile factories

Source C
Stanley Mill, Stroud, showing iron columns

Source D
Charlotte Square, Edinburgh

Activities

For this assignment you will need to study Sources A to E above and the following sources from other sections of this book: Sources A to F in Assignment 5.1 (p.33); Sources A, B, C and D in Assignment 3.2 (pp.20–21); Source C of Assignment 7.1 (p.49); and Sources A and C of Assignment 7.2 (pp.52 and 54).

1 Study Source A.

(i) Describe in your own words what happened to iron production during the period 1750 – 1850.

(ii) How do you explain the changes in iron production that are shown in Source A?

2 Study carefully Sources A to E and all the other sources that you have been asked to refer to in this assignment.

(i) What do you learn from each of these sources about the use of iron during the late 18th century and the first half of the 19th century?

(ii) Where appropriate, show how you can work out that iron was being used even if it is not actually shown in the photograph (e.g. in Source B factory chimneys show that steam power was once used. The steam engines, not shown in the photograph, would have been made of iron).

3 What other uses of iron were there during the period 1750 – 1850 that are not illustrated in these sources? In each case explain whether you think there was likely to have been an increase in the amount of iron used during this period, and for what reasons.

4 Look at the list of uses of iron that you have put down in answer to Questions 2 and 3. Which of these uses do you think consumed the largest quantities of iron? Give reasons for your answer.

5 (i) Identify in your own local area *two* fixed objects made of iron that date from the 18th or 19th centuries. Describe, draw or photograph the objects and explain when and why they were made.

(ii) Is iron used for the same purposes today? If not, why not?

Source E
Public lavatory, railway station, Melrose, Roxburghshire

Further activities

1 (i) Compare Britain in 1750 with Britain in 1850, using a grid similar to the one below:

	1750	1850
Agriculture	Most people worked on the land and lived in the countryside. Much land not enclosed. Little use of new machines.	More than 50 per cent of population living in urban areas. Most land now enclosed. Agricultural production rising fast.

(ii) To what extent was the 'industrial revolution' responsible for most of the changes that you have identified?

2 Identify *one* industrial building in your local area that dates from the period 1750-1850.

(i) Describe, draw or photograph the building and explain the purpose for which it was built.

(ii) In what ways does this building illustrate the impact of the industrial revolution?

3 Choose *three* objects in a local museum that are related in some way to industrial development during the period 1750–1850. In the case of each object, describe it carefully and show how it illustrates the impact of the industrial revolution on people's lives.

6 *Industry*
1850 to the Present Day

Compare the photograph below with the one at the beginning of Chapter 5 (p.31). Looking at these two photographs should tell you something about the changes that have taken place in British industry during the past 100 years. You must not assume of course that the first photograph is typical of the kind of industry that developed in Britain as a result of the first industrial revolution. In the same way you must not assume that the second photograph is typical of industry in late 20th century Britain. At any one time there have always been huge differences between Britain's various industries and even between one firm and another within the same industry. Major changes, however, have taken place, both in the kinds of industry that are most important in Britain and in the methods of production that these industries use. What do you learn about these changes from comparing the photograph below with the one on p.31?

The history of British industry since the last quarter of the 19th century has been one of both growth and decline: continued growth in overall production and in the development of new industries, but at the same time decline in those industries (coal, iron and steel, textiles, shipbuilding) that dominated the British economy earlier in the 19th century. The assignments in this chapter are designed to develop your understanding of these patterns of growth and decline. Assignment 6.1 looks at the last quarter of the 19th century, a period of economic growth but also a time when people first became worried about Britain's industrial decline. Assignment 6.2 focuses on the 1930s and on one particular part of the country, examining the effects of industrial change on ordinary people. The further activities suggest ways of studying the many industrial developments that have taken place since the end of the Second World War.

Assignment 6.1

Did British industry experience a 'Great Depression' in the last quarter of the 19th century?

One of the enjoyable things about studying history is that people often disagree among themselves both about what happened in the past and about why it happened. The history of British industry in the 18th and 19th centuries is no exception. There have been many disagreements among historians in recent years: about what caused the industrial revolution; about whether or not ordinary people were better off as a result of the industrial revolution; and (the subject of this assignment) about the so-called 'Great Depression' that affected British industry at the end of the 19th century. The assignment gives you some of the evidence about this so-called 'Great Depression'. It also gives you some of the statements that historians have made about it. It then encourages you to try to draw some conclusions of your own.

Source A

A dictionary definition

Economic depression: a reduction in the quality, vigour or amount of economic production and/or trade...

Source B

The growth of industrial production in Britain

Industrial production (years)	Percentage growth per annum (%)
1800–09 / 1830–39	3.1
1810–19 / 1840–49	3.5
1820–29 / 1850–59	3.5
1830–39 / 1860–69	3.0
1840–49 / 1870–79	2.9
1850–59 / 1880–89	2.4
1860–69 / 1890–99	2.1

Source C

The annual increase in manufacture per head of population (shown as a percentage). The figure 0.6 for the UK means, for example, that on average during those years manufacture (or industrial production) increased by 0.6 per cent.

	UK	Germany	USA
1871–75 / 1881–85	0.6	1.7	2.7
1881–85 / 1896–1900	0.9	3.9	2.1
1896–1900 / 1911–13	0.7	2.5	3. 2

Source D

Wholesale prices in Britain, 1815–1900. This table shows the overall rise and fall of prices during the period, not the actual prices of particular goods.

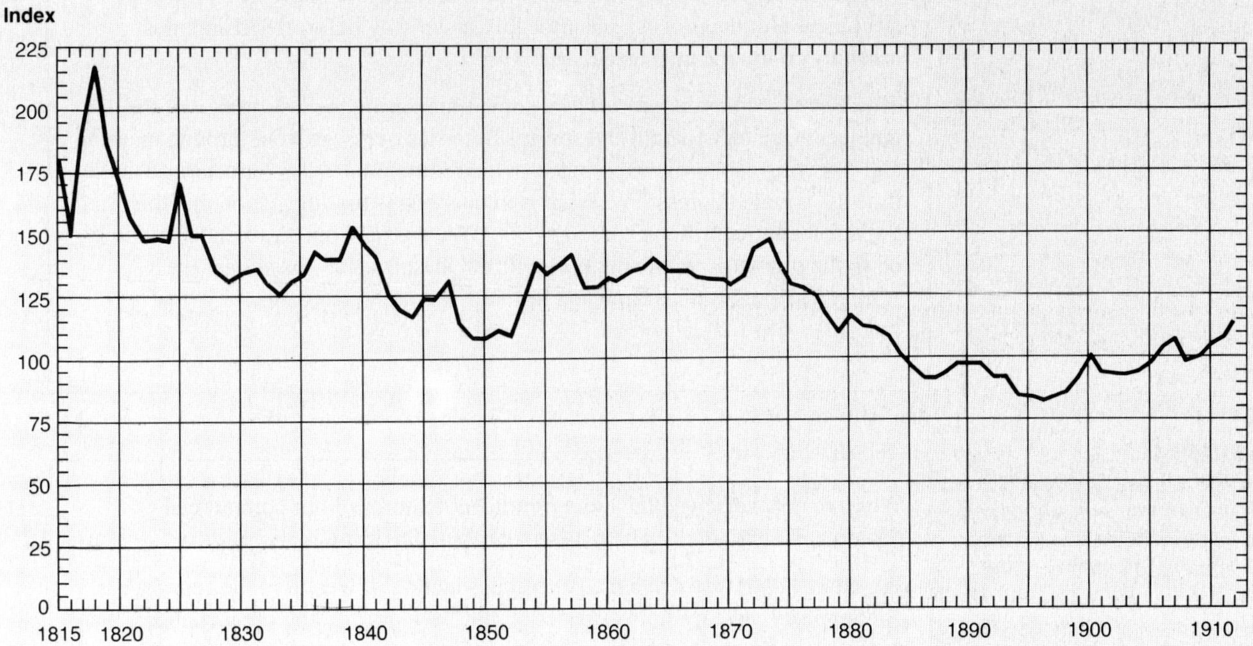

Source E

Money wages and real wages in Britain, 1850–1913. A real wage is what a money wage is able to buy in real terms, i.e. it takes into account changes in prices, rents, etc.

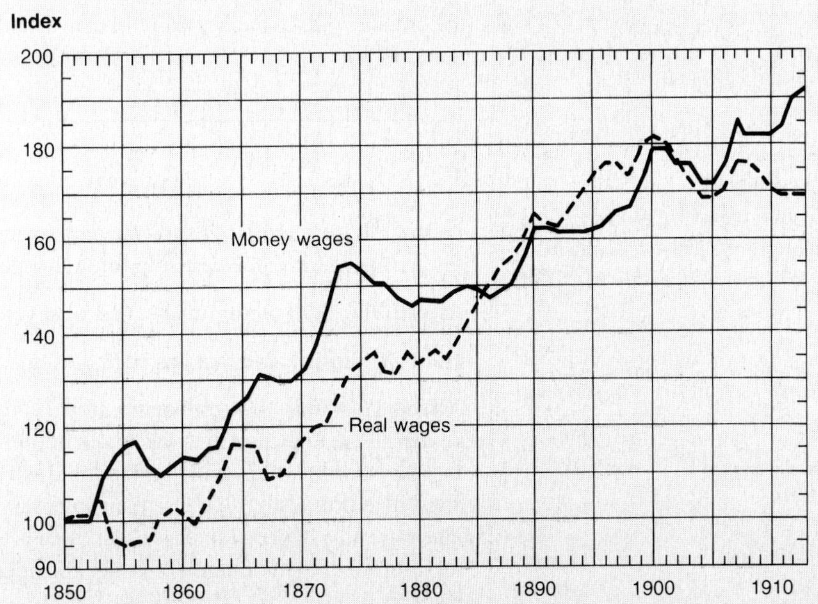

These figures make no allowance for unemployment

Source F
From S. B. Saul, *The Myth of the Great Depression 1873–1896*, 1969

As regards the "Great Depression" itself, surely the major outcome of modern research has been to destroy once and for all the idea of the existence of such a period. The last quarter or so of the nineteenth century was a watershed for Britain as competition developed overseas and the rate of growth markedly slackened. But the process was probably under way before 1870 and most certainly continued unabated... after 1900...

This is not to ignore the fact that at some time during the last quarter of the nineteenth century Britain and several countries overseas went through unusual and worrying economic experiences which sometimes they characterised at the time as "a great depression". What is in question is the suggestion that this was a special feature of the years 1873– 96 ... We are far from a full understanding of all the problems in this book. But this at least is clear: the sooner the "Great... Depression" is banished from the literature, the better.

Source G
From the *Final Report of the Royal Commission Appointed to Inquire into the Depression of Trade and Industry*, 1886

We have now reviewed the more prominent features of our commercial position, and the forces which have contributed to bring it about.

We have shown that while the general production of wealth in the country has continuously increased, its distribution has been undergoing great changes; that the result of these changes has been to give a larger share than formerly to the consumer and the labourer, and so to promote a more equal distribution; that the condition of the large class who depend upon the produce of the soil is unsatisfactory, and the number of the unemployed is a matter of serious importance; but that the general condition of the country affords encouragement for the future; that trade, though less profitable, shows little tendency to diminish in volume; but that owing to the nature of the times the demand for our commodities does not increase at the same rapid rate as formerly; that our capacity for production is consequently in excess of our requirements...; that our position as the chief manufacturing nation of the world is not so undisputed as formerly, and that foreign nations are beginning to compete with us successfully in many markets of which we formerly had a monopoly.

Source H
From a record of evidence given to the Gold and Silver Commission, 16 January 1886

Henry Chaplin (MP): Do you share the general opinion that during the last few years we have been passing through a period of severe depression?

Alfred Marshall (economist): Yes, of severe depression of profits.

Henry Chaplin: And that has been during a period of abnormally low prices?

Alfred Marshall: A severe depression of profits and of prices. I have read nearly all the evidence that was given before the Depression of Trade and Industry Commission, and I really could not see that there was any very serious attempt to prove anything else than a depression of prices, a depression of interest, and a depression of profits; there is that undoubtedly. I cannot see any reason for believing that there is any considerable depression in any other respect.

Source I
From N. Tonge and M. Quincey, *British Social and Economic History 1800–1900*, 1980

...while rejecting the notion of an economic "watershed", (historians today) acknowledge that Britain "went through an unusual and worrying economic experience" ... There is a fair measure of agreement as to the timing, 1873–96. Less certain are the causes. The following explanations have been offered:

1 Britain's early start in industrialisation became a hindrance when required to adapt to changed economic circumstances.

2 Our export trade was too narrowly based on a few staple industries.

3 The **complacency** of British **entrepreneurs**.

4 The restrictive practices of an organised labour force.

5 A system of education hostile to scientific training and social attitudes averse to 'trade'.

6 A low rate of investment in British industry.

7 The growth of foreign competition.

complacency: taking things for granted
entrepreneurs: business people

Activities

1 Study Sources A, B, C, D and E.

(i) In what ways do these sources suggest that Britain experienced an economic depression during the last quarter of the 19th century? Refer in detail to the sources in support of your answer.

(ii) In what ways do these sources suggest that Britain did not experience an economic depression?

2 Does S. B. Saul (Source F) think that there was no economic depression during the last quarter of the 19th century? Explain your answer.

3 Study Source G.

(i) Explain in your own words what Source G has to say about the state of the British economy. Number the various points 1, 2, etc.

(ii) To what extent do Sources B, C, D, E and H support the points that you have listed in your answer to (i)?

4 Do Sources A–H provide evidence to back up any of the reasons for Britain's economic problems suggested in Source I?

5 Choose *three* of the seven explanations given in Source I. Explain in what ways each of these is (or is not) a reason for Britain's economic problems. Refer to your background knowledge in support of your answer.

Assignment 6.2
The effects of industrial decline: Glasgow during the 1930s

One of the areas that suffered most from the decline of Britain's traditional industries during the inter-war years was Clydeside. This area – centred on Glasgow, Britain's second city – was heavily dependent on shipbuilding. A quick glance at Source A will show you the problems shipbuilding experienced in this area during the 1920s and 1930s. This assignment, however, is not mainly concerned with the shipbuilding industry itself. It concentrates instead on the effects of its decline on the people who lived in the area and who worked (or, in many cases, no longer worked) in the shipyards. It presents you with a range of sources of different types. One of its purposes is to get you to think about the value of these sources to someone studying life on Clydeside during this period.

Source A
From the novel *The Clydesiders* by Hugh Munro, published in 1961. The novel is set in Glasgow in the 1930s. In this passage Haig, who is unemployed, argues with Meldrum, an office worker.

If he was embarrassed Meldrum did not show it. "We're living in difficult times," he suggested. "It's all quite a problem. Even professional people are feeling the pinch."

"They'll get by." Haig was relentless. With the unyielding hatred of the unwilling dole-drawer he conceded nothing to the black-coat world. "We hear all these yarns about hard-up business folk and struggling financiers but you never meet any of them **on the Parish**. The lawyers, the doctors, the ministers— all that bunch – the newspapers make a great song about their hardships, how their stocks and shares are hardly paying enough dividends to keep them in servants and how their poor sons can hardly get a salaried job after they leave the University. Ha, it's terrible disaster if the wind blows on them! You'd think the whole world had come to an end if *they've* only two or three thousand left in the bank." Haig threw back his head and laughed satirically. Years of soured emotion found a target in the presence of this well-clad image of all the people he blamed for his misfortunes.

on the Parish: receiving poor relief

Source B
Ships launched on the River Clyde, 1918–38 (in tons)

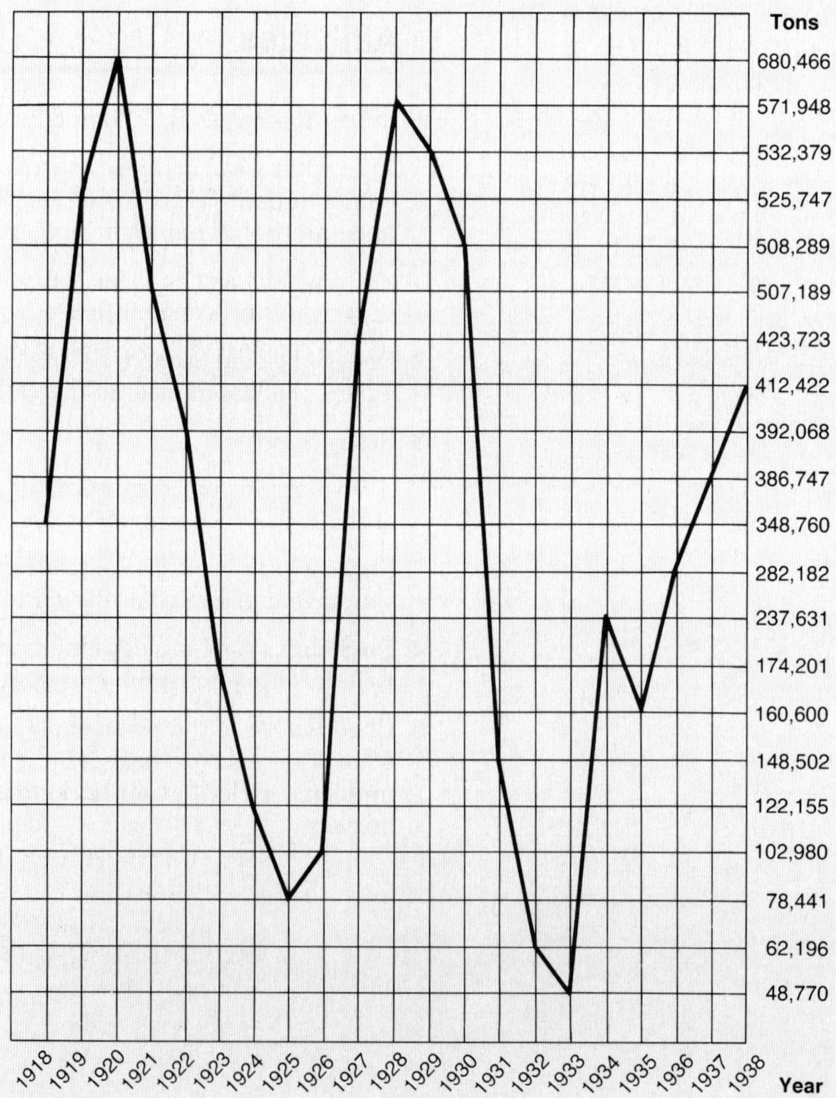

Source C

From Christopher Harvey, *No Gods and Precious Few Heroes, Scotland 1914–1980,* 1981

The Clyde's strength (was) in passenger cargo-liners and specialised ships, for which high grades of craftsmanship were required ... But the yards were constrained by old equipment and the restoration of pre-war working practices ...Until 1929 a booming American economy sustained transatlantic passenger travel ... and kept up demand for passenger liners. In 1930 Cunard-White Star laid down a £4.8m. 81,000-ton super liner. But the consequences of the Wall Street crash ended work on "No.534" (the *Queen Mary)* at Clydebank. Elsewhere, orders dried up; by 1933 Scottish output, at 74,000 tons, was lower than in the 1850s. In February 1930 Sir James Lithgow and the Bank of England set up the National Shipbuilders' Security Corporation to "rationalize" the industry by buying up ... under-used yards. It had cut capacity 15–20 per cent by 1935 – at the cost of great unpopularity– but by then work was resumed on the *Queen Mary* (completed 1936). Cunard laid down a sister ship, and the government started to subsidise cargo steamer construction. Overshadowing everything, rearmament brought, between 1935 and 1939, £80m. worth of arms orders. But the underlying problems of the industry remained as far from solution as ever.

Source D

From the novel *No Mean City* by A. McArthur and R. Kingsley Long, published in 1954. The novel is set in Glasgow in the 1930s. This extract describes the thoughts of a character known as John Stark as he lay in bed at night in his two-room tenement flat.

Blending with the other smells of the house was the reek of paraffin. It was particularly strong in the **cavity bed** when the door was shut, for the woodwork was infested with bugs and Stark's wife conscientiously tried to keep them under by smearing every crack with oil.

And yet, even in her sleep, he could feel her scratching. The movements of her arm exasperated him almost beyond endurance. He would have shaken her and told her to lie still if it had not been for the baby, not yet six months old.

Being out of work and on the dole as he was, another child was not a financial burden. Two shillings was allowed for the baby and it scarcely cost as much as that. But as he lay there in the darkness he wondered grimly how it was that all the women in the slums seemed to want kids, even Annie, over forty and with seven living...

John Stark began to feel drowsy. He could hear his dead brother's daughter, Maggie, snoring in the "shake-doon" beyond the fireplace. The girl always slept with her mouth wide open and her nose was small, with pinched nostrils. She ought to have been sent to the hospital when she was young. Still, she was bringing in three-and-sixpence a week now from the carpet factory.

He thought of his neighbours, the Hurleys, who had recently found a good lodger. The Hurleys were almost as crowded as the Starks, but they were lucky, because their lodger was a night-worker, and so there was always a bed free for him in the day ...

cavity bed: a bed in a kind of cupboard, common in Glasgow flats of this period

Source E

A second extract from the novel *No Mean City*

Communism, of a sort, was preached at many a street corner, but the **Gorbals** jeered at the politicians. They did not believe in any of them. They thought them all a lot of grafters, scrambling for office, glib of promise, empty of performance. Voting "Red" because the offered bribe was bigger, they sneered as they made their crosses on the ballot papers. They cared for nothing – literally nothing – except the rate of **outdoor relief** and the faint hope of a reduction in the rent or a bigger allowance to meet this burden.

Some of the slum-dwellers were "Prodisants" and the others "Catholics", but not one in ten thought of his religion as anything but a label or banner to fight under. They were contemptuous alike of God and their fellow men. They despised their own City Council more than they despised Westminster. The Glasgow Municipal Buildings were commonly known among them as the "Chamber of Horrors" or the "House of Corruption" ...

Gorbals: slum district of Glasgow
outdoor relief: the dole

Source F

References to Glasgow in newspapers published during the 1930s

wards: areas
cliques: groups
insignia of office: the things that they carry that show what their job is

News of the World, 29 April 1934

It is not uncommon for eight, ten, or twelve persons to be herded together in a single room. There are (in Glasgow) 175,000 "houses" without baths, and 105,000 "houses" have no internal sanitation.

Daily Herald, 16 March 1934

Glasgow's infantile death rate, which was mainly caused by tenement congestion, was 112 in the thousand in 1932 compared with 67 per thousand in London and Birmingham. The infantile death rate in tenement **wards** is four to six times greater than in residential areas where there are few tenements.

Sunday Express, 3 March 1935

The gangsters *have* come to Britain. Glasgow, second city of the Empire ... frankly acknowledges their reign of terror. A thousand young men – not forty are more than thirty-five – rule the poorer class districts. Their **insignia of office** are the broken bottle, the razor blade, the "cosh", the knife, and – newest and most effective of all – the bayonet.

The Sunday Mail, 3 February 1935

During the last ten years, in Glasgow alone, gangsterdom has been responsible for at least four slayings and the serious injuring and maiming of many others who have incurred the savage wrath of the different **cliques** of young hooligans who terrorise the poorer districts of the city ... In true Chicago style the Glasgow gangster has his "Moll", and in (the dance halls where gangsters meet up) she is frequently the cause of the trouble that leads to razor-slashed faces and bottle-crowned heads ...

Activities

1. How bad was the economic depression that affected Glasgow during the 1930s, and what were its causes? Extract information from Sources B and C that will help you to answer this question.
2. Study Sources A, D and E. What questions would you need to ask before using these sources as evidence for ways of life in Glasgow during the 1930s?
3. Do Sources A, D and E illustrate the impact of the economic depression on Glasgow? Explain your answer.
4. What other features of Glasgow life, not the result of the depression, are reflected in Sources A, D and E?
5. Are the extracts in Source F more useful to someone studying Glasgow life in the 1930s than the novels quoted in Sources A, D and E? Explain your answer.

Further activities

1. Choose any *two* of the following decades: 1850s; 1890s; 1930s; 1950s; 1980s. Compare the state of British industry in the two decades that you have chosen.
2. What were the effects on British industry of *either* the First World War *or* the Second World War?
3. Find out as much as you can about the development of industry in your own local area during the last 100 years. Write an account of how industry has changed during this period, giving reasons for the changes that have taken place.
4. During the 1980s many people talked about Britain experiencing another 'industrial revolution' as a result of developments in information technology. Describe the developments in information technology that took place during that decade and explain the effects that they have had.

7 *The Transport Revolution*

The industrial revolution, the agricultural changes of the 18th and early 19th centuries, and the growth in Britain's population all had one consequence in common: a growing demand for improvements in transport. In 1750 methods of transport had hardly changed for centuries. Within the next 100 years they were to be transformed through the construction of better road surfaces and through the creation of networks of canals and railways. The main stimulus was the need for cheaper and faster transport for goods, for agricultural produce and industrial raw materials, as well as for finished goods.

The assignments in this chapter look at two aspects of this 'transport revolution': the construction of canals and the building of one of Britain's earliest railways. The main concern of the first assignment (7.1) is with how the canals were constructed and with the experiences of those involved in their construction. The second assignment (7.2) focuses on the motives of the early railway builders and on the nature of railway transport in its early stages. The further activities at the end of the chapter suggest ways in which you might explore the effects that changes in transport had on the British economy and on the way of life of the British people.

Building the London to Birmingham Railway, 1837

Assignment 7.1
Navvies and the building of the canals

The Bridgewater Canal, built by James Brindley for the Duke of Bridgewater and opened in 1761, was not the first canal to be built in England. It was this canal however that succeeded in capturing people's imagination, mainly because financially it was an immediate success. By creating a direct link between Manchester and the Duke's coal mines near Worsley, the Bridgewater Canal greatly reduced the cost of transportation. This benefited both producer and consumer – the producer because of increased profits and the consumer because of reduced prices.

The success of the Bridgewater Canal encouraged others to follow suit. During the next 20 years there was a spate of canal building: the Grand Trunk Canal, linking the Trent and the Mersey; an extension linking the Bridgewater Canal with the Mersey; the Staffordshire and Worcestershire Canal; the Birmingham Canal; the Oxford Canal. Most of these were equally successful. Their success led to further ventures during the 1790s and the early 19th century – the period of the so-called 'canal mania', during which large numbers of acts of parliament were passed permitting the building of a great many canals. By 1830, when most of the building had come to an end, approximately 6500 km had been added to Britain's navigable waterways.

The canals had many important effects. They played a major part in stimulating and making possible the growth of British industry. They improved the supply of goods to consumers at home. They also brought substantial profits to many of the people who had invested in them. Unlike railways however they were not widely used for transporting passengers.

One effect, especially noticeable while they were being built, was the creation of a lot of new jobs. At a time when there were few, if any, machines to aid construction, canal building required large numbers of labourers. These were known as the 'navvies' – from 'navigation', the 18th century word for canal. This assignment looks at the work of these navvies and at the attitudes of other people towards them. It also looks at the people who worked on the canals once they were built.

Source A

An advertisement in the Bath Chronicle, 5 July 1804

To CANAL DIGGERS, etc.

WANTED, Six or Eight Hundred Men, to be immediately employed in Cutting the NEW DOCKS and CANAL for Improving the HARBOUR of BRISTOL, where every encouragement will be given to men, and the prices **as under** for some or greater part of the works, viz. $3^1/_2$d. and in some places 4d. per yard, for the first stage of 20 yards, and 1d. per yard for every 20 yards in length after the first 20 yards; and 3d. per yard for filling Carts. To receive Four Shillings per day subsistence, and a final settlement every month. The ground consists of clay and silt, and the materials are all ready for that number of men. Men coming from great distance shall receive something for their travelling expences.

as under: as stated below

Source B

From S. Shaw, *A Journey to the West of England in 1788,* 1789

We now approached the great tunnel, which forms part of the communication between the Severn and the Thames ... one end penetrates the hill at the village of Sapperton, the other comes out in Heywood; we turned on our left to visit the former and saw the shafts busy in several places, at a distance of about 230 yards from each other; by this means they wind up the material from the cavity and **expedite** the work. The earth is principally a hard blue marle, and in some places quite a rock which they blow up with gun-powder, the depth of these pits are upon an average eighty yards from the surface. The first contractor receives £7 per yard from the company, and the labourers rent it at the rate of about £3 per yard, finding candles, gunpowder, etc., the workers are in eight gangs, having two or three reliefs and continue eight hours at a time, day and night.

expedite: speed up

Source C

Trent and Mersey Canal, Shardlow, Derbyshire

Source D

From the *Taunton Gazette*, 27 April 1811

On Monday last a disturbance, of a serious nature, occurred at Sampford Peverell. The annual fair, for the sale of cattle, etc., was held there on that day. On the Saturday preceding, a number of the workmen employed in excavating the bed of the Grand Western Canal assembled at Wellington for the purpose of obtaining change for the payment of their wages, which there has been lately considerable difficulty in **procuring**. Many of them engaged in **inordinate** drinking, and committed various excesses at Tiverton, and other places to which they had gone for the purpose above stated. On Monday (at) the fair at Sampford ... much rioting took place in the course of the day, and towards evening a body of these men, consisting of not less than 300, had assembled in the village. Mr. Chave (a local gentleman) ... was met on the road, and recognised by some of the party. **Opprobrious** language was applied to him ... The rioters followed him to the house, the windows of which they broke; and apprehensive of further violence, Mr. Chave considered it necessary to his defence to discharge a loaded pistol at the assailants. This unfortunately took effect, and one man fell dead on the spot.

procuring: obtaining
inordinate: excessive
opprobrious: offensive

Source E

From D. D. Gladwin, *The Waterways of Britain*, 1976

Up to the end of the first quarter of the nineteenth century there was an inadequate supply of small coinage ... partially because insufficient was minted to meet the demand ... One result ... was the issue of copper tokens – only exchangeable at the Tommy Shop or Public House— often by the canal company or one of the proprietors.

Source F
From J. Hassell, *Tour of the Grand Junction Navigation*, 1819

... a watchman's cottage belonging to the Canal Company, whose occupation is partly to prevent the navigators from **committing depredations** in their passage through the park; for which purpose a vista is cut through the plantations, so that a view of the boats may be distinctly had, during their passing from hence to the fisherman's cottage at the opposite extremity of the park, and vice versa.

committing depredations: causing damage/thieving

Source G
From W. Hutton, *An History of Birmingham*, 1781

The boats are nearly alike, constructed to fit the locks, carry about 25 tons, and are each drawn by something like the skeleton of a horse covered with skin; whether he subsists upon the scent of the water, is a doubt; but whether his life is a scene of affliction is not; for the unfeeling driver has no employment but to whip him from one end of the canal to the other ... We can scarcely view a boat travelling this liquid road without raising opposite sensations – pleased to think of its great benefit to the community and grieved to behold **wanton** punishment.

wanton: cruel and pointless

Activities

1 What do you learn from Sources A and B about the construction methods used in building the canals?

2 Using your background knowledge, identify any other construction problems encountered by the canal builders and describe the ways in which they tried to solve them.

3 What do you learn from Sources A and B about the way in which navvies were employed? Answer in your own words.

4 'As well as employing large numbers of navvies, the canals also gave work to many others.' What other kinds of work are suggested by the part of the canal shown in Source C?

5 In what ways does Source E help to explain some of the events described in Source D?

6 (i) How reliable are Sources D, F and G as evidence for the attitudes and behaviour of navvies and canal boatmen?

(ii) Many people at the time regarded navvies and canal boatmen as a dangerous, violent and undisciplined group of people. Do Sources D, F and G suggest that they deserved this reputation?

7 Investigate the way of life of canal boatpeople during the 18th and 19th centuries. In what respects did their way of life differ from that of other working people at the time?

Assignment 7.2
The opening of the Liverpool and Manchester Railway, 1830

The Liverpool and Manchester Railway, opened in 1830, has been described as 'the first modern railway'. All the features that had been tried out on earlier railways were combined here for the first time: the use of steam power; services for both passengers and goods; a regular timetable; and services provided exclusively by the company that owned the railway. It was an immediate success and stimulated the formation of railway companies in many other parts of the country.

The Liverpool and Manchester Railway was a triumph for the engineering skills of George and Robert Stephenson. George Stephenson overcame the many obstacles involved in taking the railway across a great marsh, over a valley and through deep cuttings and tunnels. His son Robert's locomotive, the Rocket, beat all its rivals at the Rainhill trials in 1829 and was thus used as the locomotive for the new railway. Robert Stephenson went on to engineer the London and Birmingham Railway, approved by parliament in 1833 and opened in 1838.

This assignment examines the motives of those who promoted the Liverpool and Manchester Railway. It also looks at some of the contemporary sources relating to the opening of the railway. These sources can tell us a great deal about the attitudes of the people who took part.

Source A

A contemporary illustration of the Liverpool and Manchester Railway, showing the scene at Edge Hill, Liverpool, on the morning of opening day (15 September 1830)

Source B

From the prospectus issued by the Committee of the Liverpool and Manchester Railroad Company, announcing its intention of promoting a railway between Liverpool and Manchester (quoted in T. Baines, *History of Liverpool,* 1852)

The total quantity of **merchandise** passing between Liverpool and Manchester is estimated, by the lowest computation, at 1,100 tons per day. The bulk of this merchandise is transported either by the Duke of Bridgwater's Canal or the "Mersey and Irwell Navigation". By both of these **conveyances** goods must pass up the river Mersey, a distance of 16 or 18 miles, subject to serious delays from contrary winds and not infrequently to actual loss or damage from **tempestuous** weather. The average length of passage, by these conveyances, including the **customary** detention on the wharfs, may be taken at 36 hours ... The average charge upon merchandise for the last 14 years has been about 15s. a ton.

By the projected railroad, the transit of merchandise between Liverpool and Manchester will be effected in 4 or 5 hours, and the charge to the merchant will be reduced at least one-third. Here, then will be accomplished an immense **pecuniary** saving to the public, over and above what is perhaps still more important, the economy of time ... It will afford stimulus to the productive industry of the country ...

But it is not altogether on account of the exorbitant charges of the water-carriers that a railroad is desirable. The present canal establishments are inadequate to ... the regular and punctual conveyance of goods at all periods and seasons. In summer time there is frequently a deficiency of water, obliging boats to go only half-loaded, while, in winter, they are sometimes locked up with frosts, for weeks together ...

In addition to the transport of goods between Liverpool and Manchester, an important branch of **revenue** may be expected to result to the proprietors of the projected road, from the conveyance of coals from the rich mines in the vicinity of St Helens ... These coals at present pass along the Sankey Canal, and down the Mersey to Liverpool ...

Amongst the widely-diffused benefits to be expected from the proposed railroad, must especially be enumerated, no inconsiderable advance in the commercial prosperity of Ireland ...

The immediate and prominent advantages to be derived from the proposed railroad are, increased facilities to the general operations of commerce, arising out of that punctuality and dispatch which will attend the transit of merchandise between Liverpool and Manchester, as well as immense pecuniary saving to the trading community ... Moreover, as a cheap and **expeditious** means of conveyance for travellers, the railway holds out the fair prospect of a public accommodation, the magnitude and importance of which cannot be immediately ascertained ...

merchandise: goods
conveyances: methods of transport
tempestuous: stormy
customary: usual
pecuniary: financial
revenue: income/money
expeditious: fast

Source C
A medal commemorating the opening of the Liverpool and Manchester Railway, issued at the time

Source D
From an account by M. Sturge Gretton written in the 20th century

My grandfather who was ... one of the guests of the Liverpool and Manchester Railway on the occasion of the running of their first passenger train, used to recount how the Duke of Wellington, who was also a guest, became plastered with mud in his efforts to shield the ladies from the filth that the populace, ranged along the line, was flinging at the travellers.

Source E
From an account by Fanny Kemble written in the mid-19th century

The vast concourse of people who had assembled (in Manchester) to witness the arrival of the successful travellers, was of the lowest order of mechanics and artisans, among whom great distress and a dangerous spirit of discontent with the Government at that time prevailed. Groans and hisses greeted the carriageful of influential personages in which the Duke of Wellington sat ... High above the grim and grimy crowd of smiling faces a loom had been erected at which a tattered, starved-looking weaver, evidently set there as a representative man, to protest against the triumph of machinery, and the gain and the glory which the wealthy Liverpool and Manchester men were likely to derive from it.

Activities

1 Study Source A.

(i) How would you explain (a) the large barrels and (b) the high walls shown in this scene?

(ii) Does this source suggest that the opening of the railway was greeted with great enthusiasm? Give reasons for your answer.

2 Study Source B.

(i) Why do you think the authors of Source B issued this prospectus?

(ii) What, according to the authors of Source B, would be the benefits of the proposed Liverpool and Manchester Railway? Answer in your own words.

3 Study Source C. Why do you think this particular scene was chosen for a commemorative medal? Explain your answer.

4 Study Sources D and E.

(i) Do you learn anything about the attitudes of these two authors? Refer to the sources in support of your answer.

(ii) Are these sources likely to give a reliable account of the opening of the railway? Explain your answer.

(iii) Why do you think the people mentioned in these sources were so hostile?

5 Re-read your answer to Question 2 (ii). Were the authors of Source B correct in claiming that the railways would bring great benefits to the country? Refer to the period 1830 – 50.

Further activities

1 Was there a revolution in *all* methods of transport during the period 1750 – 1850? Support your answer by specific references to developments in different kinds of transport.

2 Using old maps, local history books, and the evidence on the ground, investigate the development of *one* kind of transport in your own area during the period 1750–1870. Possible areas of investigation are: roads and road transport; canals and rivers; railways; transport by sea. In writing up the results of your investigation, comment on the ways in which your area was affected by these developments.

3 Choose *two* features in your local area that relate to transport during the period 1750–1870, e.g. a toll cottage, a canal lock, a bridge, a railway station, a coach house. Draw or photograph both features and write a short account explaining what you learn from them about life during this period.

4 What effect did the railways have on the way people spent their leisure time? Refer to the period 1830–70.

5 Museums contain many objects that relate to transport during the last two centuries. You have studied one of these – from the National Railway Museum in York – in Assignment 7.1. Choose *one* object in a museum that is connected with transport during the period 1750–1870, e.g. a coach, toll sign, sedan chair, medal, railway poster, canal token, etc. Study the object carefully and write a brief report describing it in detail and explaining what you learn from it about transport during the period to which it relates.

8 *Transport and Communications*
since 1870

Look at the advertisements in Source A. These were printed in *The Times* newspaper during the 1870s. Then compare them with the advertisements in Source B – from the same newspaper over 100 years later. This gives you some idea of the extent to which transport changed during this period. These changes have had major consequences both for Britain and for the whole world.

Source A

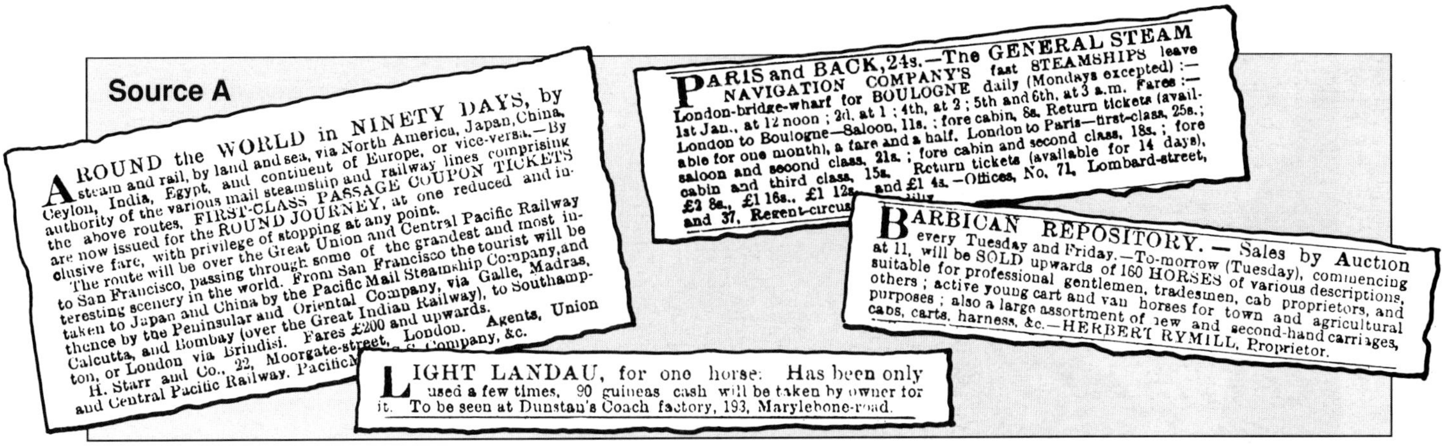
AROUND the WORLD in NINETY DAYS, by steam and rail, by land and sea, via North America, Japan, China, Ceylon, India, Egypt, and continent of Europe, or vice-versa.—By authority of the various mail steamship and railway lines comprising the above routes, FIRST-CLASS PASSAGE COUPON TICKETS are now issued for the ROUND JOURNEY, at one reduced and inclusive fare, with privilege of stopping at any point.
The route will be over the Great Union and Central Pacific Railway to San Francisco, passing through some of the grandest and most interesting scenery in the world. From San Francisco the tourist will be taken to Japan and China by the Pacific Mail Steamship Company, and thence by the Peninsular and Oriental Company, via Galle, Madras, Calcutta, and Bombay (over the Great Indian Railway), to Southampton, or London via Brindisi. Fares £200 and upwards. Agents, Union H. Starr and Co., 22, Moorgate-street, London. Pacific … Company, &c. and Central Pacific Railway.

PARIS and BACK, 24s.—The GENERAL STEAM NAVIGATION COMPANY'S fast STEAMSHIPS leave London-bridge-wharf for BOULOGNE daily (Mondays excepted) :— 1st Jan., at 12 noon ; 3d, at 1 ; 4th, at 2 ; 5th and 6th, at 3 a.m. Fares :— London to Boulogne—Saloon, 11s. ; fore cabin, 8s. Return tickets (available for one month), a fare and a half. London to Paris—first-class, 25s. ; saloon and second class, 21s. ; fore cabin and second class, 18s. ; fore cabin and third class, 15s. Return tickets (available for 14 days), £2 8s., £1 16s., £1 12s., and £1 4s.—Offices, No. 71, Lombard-street, and 37, Regent-circus …

BARBICAN REPOSITORY.— Sales by Auction every Tuesday and Friday.—To-morrow (Tuesday), commencing at 11, will be SOLD upwards of 160 HORSES of various descriptions, suitable for professional gentlemen, tradesmen, cab proprietors, and others ; active young cart and van horses for town and agricultural purposes ; also a large assortment of new and second-hand carriages, cabs, carts, harness, &c.—HERBERT RYMILL, Proprietor.

LIGHT LANDAU, for one horse: Has been only used a few times. 90 guineas cash will be taken by owner for it. To be seen at Dunstan's Coach factory, 193, Marylebone-road.

In many ways these changes were even more of a 'transport revolution' than the railway revolution of the first half of the 19th century. Perhaps their single most important cause was the development of the internal combustion engine. This revolutionised land transport, making possible the motor car, motor bicycle, motor bus and lorry. It also led to engine-powered flight and the growth of the aircraft industry.

Other major influences have been the growing use of electricity, the application of new developments in electronics, and the introduction of methods of mass production. As with other economic and social changes discussed in this book, the two world wars also stimulated transport developments in many different ways, for example the use of lorries in World War I and the introduction of radar in World War II.

The first assignment (8.1) in this chapter helps you to study some of the developments that have taken place in road transport during this period. It also examines the effects of these developments on people's way of life. Suggestions for ways of investigating other aspects of land, air and sea transport are given at the end of the chapter.

Mass production, the growing use of electricity, the application of electronics, the impact of war – all these factors have helped to revolutionise other aspects of communications during the 20th century. The introduction (or development) of telephones, radio, films, television, computers, and new methods of printing has helped to transform both the British economy and the way of life of ordinary people. The second assignment (8.2) looks at one of the most important of these developments – something that we take for granted but the introduction of which has made the world a very different place.

Source B

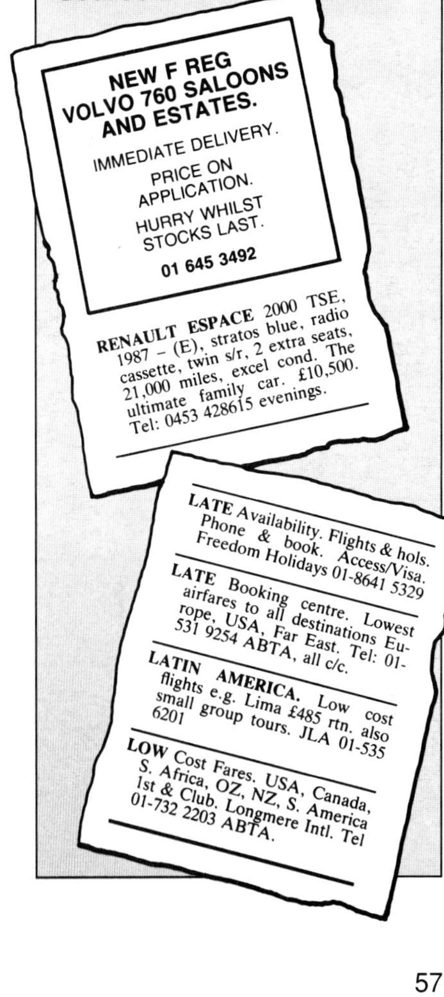
NEW F REG VOLVO 760 SALOONS AND ESTATES.
IMMEDIATE DELIVERY.
PRICE ON APPLICATION.
HURRY WHILST STOCKS LAST.
01 645 3492

RENAULT ESPACE 2000 TSE, 1987 – (E), stratos blue, radio cassette, twin s/r, 2 extra seats, 21,000 miles, excel cond. The ultimate family car. £10,500. Tel: 0453 428615 evenings.

LATE Availability. Flights & hols. Phone & book. Access/Visa. Freedom Holidays 01-8641 5329

LATE Booking centre. Lowest airfares to all destinations Europe, USA, Far East. Tel: 01-531 9254 ABTA, all c/c.

LATIN AMERICA. Low cost flights e.g. Lima £485 rtn. also small group tours. JLA 01-535 6201

LOW Cost Fares. USA, Canada, S. Africa, OZ, NZ, S. America 1st & Club. Longmere Intl. Tel 01-732 2203 ABTA.

Assignment 8.1
Road transport in the 20th century

The main aim of this assignment is to get you to think about changes in road transport in the 20th century: why they took place and the effects they have had. The last part of the assignment encourages you to apply your understanding of this topic to a study of some of these developments in your own local area. All four photographs were taken in the Yorkshire town of Huddersfield.

Source C
Buxton Road, Huddersfield, *circa* 1925 (*circa* means around the time of – the exact date of the photograph is not known)

Source D
John William Street, Huddersfield, *circa* 1930

Source E
Buxton Road, Huddersfield, 1962

Source F
The Ramsden Canal, Huddersfield, 1953

Activities

1 Study Sources A and B.

(i) What do you learn from Sources A and B about the differences in transport between the 1870s and the 1980s?

(ii) What other differences between the 1870s and the 1980s are illustrated in these sources?

2 Study Sources C, D and E.

(i) Identify *six* kinds of road transport shown in these photographs.

(ii) Which of these methods of transport were in general use in Britain (a) in 1850, (b) in 1890, (c) in 1914, and (d) in 1950? Refer to your textbook in order to find the answers.

3 Choose *two* of the methods of transport that you identified in Question 2 (*exclude* the one that was already in existence in 1850).

(i) In each case explain why this method of transport developed at the time that it did.

(ii) In each case describe the effects of the introduction of this method of transport. In answering this question, try to think of as many effects as you can, e.g. on the economy, on people's leisure activities, on where people lived, on the environment, etc.

4 Study Sources C, D, E and F.

(i) Is there anything in these sources to suggest that changes in transport were often gradual? Refer in detail to the sources.

(ii) Can you think of any reasons why transport changes often took place very gradually?

5 Give an account of the development in your own local area of *one* of the new methods of transport shown in Sources C, D and E. In the course of your answer describe any effects that this method of transport has had.

Assignment 8.2
Amusing ourselves to death: the impact of television

Amusing Ourselves to Death is the title of a recent book on television and its effect on people. The author believes that television has the effect of turning the whole of life into an entertainment – of making even the most serious things seem trivial. He is alarmed at the way in which television seems to destroy our ability to think for ourselves. In his opinion its effect in the end is to take away our freedom. Many people of course would disagree, but views like these are worth thinking about. They are part of a general concern, shared by many people, about the way in which television has changed our lives and how we look at the world.

However much we might disagree about its effects, no one could deny that the introduction of television has been one of the most important changes of the 20th century. This assignment looks at some of the main stages in the development of television and then examines its impact on people's attitudes and way of life.

Source A

From James Curran and Jean Seton, *Power Without Responsibility, The Press and Broadcasting in Britain,* 1985

The opposition to commercial television was organized by the National Television Council ...This group objected to the cultural consequences of commercial television – it would "vulgarise ... and coarsen" wrote one critic.

The argument became more fierce when it was learnt that in America the Coronation had been shown interspersed with NBC's television chimp, J. Fred Muggs, selling tea. A deodorant had been advertised just before the **ritual anointment.** Horrified MPs suggested that if a commercial system were started here, royal tours would be interrupted by commercial breaks (advertising) the makers of the Queen's chairs and carpets.

Nevertheless the Act introducing commercial television was passed in 1954 because most Tories believed that in some way it would promote industry, commerce and the free market.

ritual anointment: the solemn moment in the Coronation service when the Queen was anointed (or smeared) with holy oil

Source B

Extracts from an unpublished diary kept by a woman, aged 31, in August 1942. The writer had recently married and was living with her mother in Stoke-on-Trent. Her husband was on military service.

SATURDAY 8TH *... This afternoon Betty and I went to Hanley to the Odeon to see Bob Hope and Madeleine Carroll in* My Favourite Blonde *– a few funny passages ...*

FRIDAY 14TH *... went to Crewe with Betty to see* One of our Bombers is Missing *– a good picture – amusing too – nothing like its title leads you to believe ...*

SATURDAY 15TH *... Went to the Hippodrome at night to see Robert Taylor in* Johnny Eager *– I wasn't very thrilled – neither was Lal – still we can't always pick winners can we?*

MONDAY 17TH *... Done a lot of sewing on Patricia's little frock, then Mum and Auntie Stevens and I played Rummy – Mum won.*

WEDNESDAY 19TH *... Mum met Mary at 4.30 p.m. and they had tea then I met them outside the Odeon and we saw* Reap the Wild Wind *– in technicolour.*

THURSDAY 20TH *... played "500 up" with Mum and Auntie Stevens (Mum won) and another "300 up" when Auntie Eym joined us – she's sleeping here – Uncle is firewatching – my turn tomorrow.*

SATURDAY 22ND *... Met Mary in Stoke and came home to lunch then with Mum we went to the Majestic to see* The Maltese Falcon *with Mary Astor and Humphrey Bogart – a real brain teaser and* The Smiling Ghost, *an amusing "spooky".*

SUNDAY 23RD *... Auntie and Mr Stevens are coming in soon for "500 up" – he really enjoys a game of cards with us.*

THURSDAY 27TH *... Also played "500 up" with Mum and Auntie Stevens tonight – Auntie won this time. Now I think I'll take the portable wireless to bed with me.*

Source C

Leisure tastes by sex and age in England and Wales, 1978. The figures show the percentage of the evening spent by each group in the various activities that are listed.

	Female					Male				
Activites	**18–24**	**25–35**	**35–54**	**54+**	**All ages**	**18–24**	**25–34**	**35–54**	**54+**	**All ages**
Domestic etc.	12.8	19.9	20.9	16.2	18.5	10.7	18.9	19.5	13.5	16.7
Drinking activites	13.2	4.2	4.2	1.9	4.5	26.4	14.0	13.2	6.9	12.9
Social activities away from home	25.3	21.0	19.2	12.9	18.0	31.2	19.2	16.2	10.4	16.4
Social activities at home	6.0	6.0	7.2	6.0	6.0	3.0	7.2	6.0	6.2	6.0
Watching TV	42.8	48.9	48.5	63.0	53.0	28.7	40.7	45.1	63.0	48.0

Source: *Social Trends*, 1982

Source D

Changes in cinema attendance and in the percentage of the population with television sets

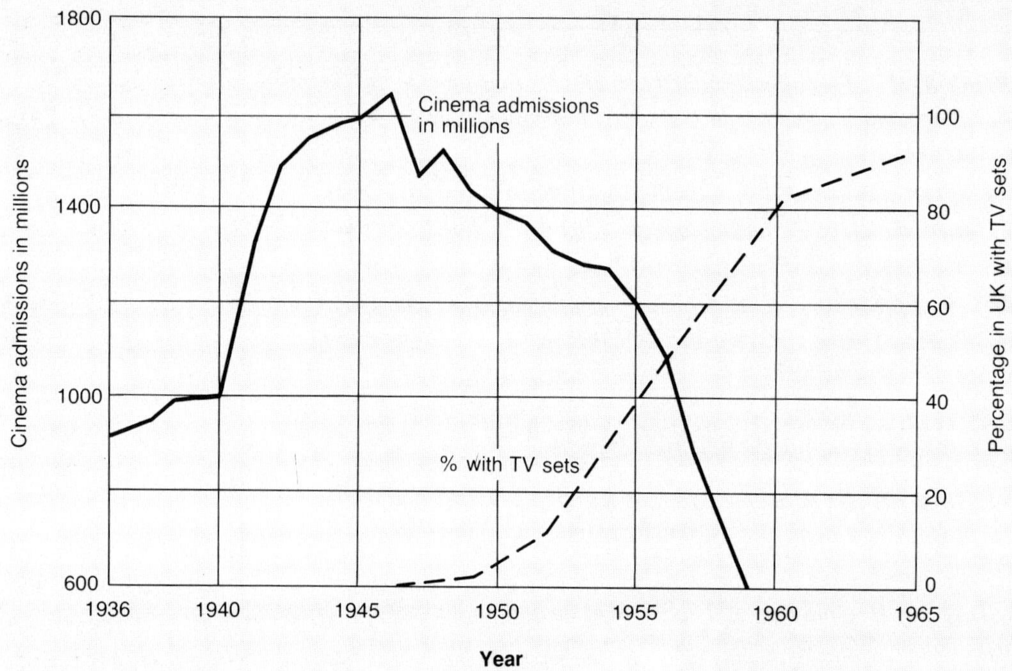

Source E

From James Curran and Jean Seton, *Power Without Responsibility, The Press and Broadcasting in Britain,* 1985

... following an American trend, the number of "live" television viewing hours per British inhabitant has actually declined. Between 1980 and 1983 average viewing in Britain dropped by as much as one and a half hours per week, with particularly large reductions during bank holidays when ratings are normally highest. Christmas 1982 saw a staggering 22 per cent average drop since the previous December, with barely any recovery a year later.

... part of the reason is the parallel growth of video: time previously spent on current programmes is now devoted to video cassettes.

Source F

From Stuart Hood, *A Survey of Television,* 1967

... too much (of the children's programmes) is second rate: inadequately dubbed Fench films, desperately boring importations from Eastern Europe and the German Democratic Republic. Pop programmes are highly successful. America sends cartoons which range from the brilliant to the worst kind of Disneyism and telefilms of varying quality. What is lacking is British or Commonwealth adventure films which would provide children with the kind of storytelling they enjoy and need.

Activities

1 Use your background knowledge.

(i) Describe the part played by each of the following developments in the history of British television since 1945: the introduction of the videotape recorder; communications satellites; mass-produced transistorised sets; colour television; the ending of the BBC monopoly in 1955.

(ii) Is it possible to choose one of these developments as the one that has had the biggest effect on the development of television? Explain your answer.

2 Using both Source A and any background knowledge, give reasons why (a) the Conservative government passed the Act referred to in Source A, and (b) the Labour Party and many others opposed this Act.

3 Study Sources B, C, D and E.

(i) What do you learn from Source B about the ways in which the writer spent her spare time?

(ii) Do Sources C, D and E suggest that during the post-war years television has largely put an end to leisure activities of this kind? Explain your answer, referring in detail to the sources.

4 'In some ways television has weakened people's sense of identity. In other ways it has perhaps strengthened it.'

(i) Explain in your own words what this statement means.

(ii) Does Source F support this statement? Explain your answer.

(iii) Do you agree with this statement? Back up your answer with evidence.

5 What *other* effects has television had on Britain since 1945? Refer to television's effects on politics, on the economy, and on people's attitudes.

Further activities

1 (i) Describe the main changes that have taken place in Britain since 1870 in *one* of the following: rail transport; sea transport; aviation.

(ii) What reasons help to explain these changes?

(iii) What have been the effects of these changes?

2 (i) Use old road maps to give an account of the development of motorways in Britain.

(ii) Why were motorways built in these places and at those times?

(iii) What have been the effects of motorways on the British economy and the British way of life?

3 Interview *three* people (born before 1945) about the changes in transport that have taken place during their lifetimes. Write a brief report comparing the experiences of the three people and summarising what you have learnt from the interviews. In the course of your answer try to comment on the extent to which you think this kind of oral evidence is reliable.

4 Interview someone (born before 1945) who has worked in offices for much of his or her working life. Try to find out how offices have changed in the course of his or her lifetime. How do these changes illustrate the major changes in communications that have taken place during the second half of the 20th century? In the course of your answer try to comment on the extent to which you think this kind of oral evidence is reliable.

9 *Britain's Overseas Trade*

Long before the period covered by this book Britain had depended for its livelihood on trading links with the outside world. The existence of overseas markets played an important part in stimulating the industrial developments referred to in Chapter 5. Overseas trade also provided the capital (i.e. money) that was needed for investment in industry and transport.

Once the industrial revolution was underway, Britain's dependence on overseas trade was even greater. A large proportion of the country's manufactured goods ended up as exports. Britain became the 'workshop of the world'. It also became more and more dependent on the import of raw materials for its new industries. British shipping – exporting manufactured goods and importing raw materials – dominated the sea lanes of the world.

During the late 18th and early 19th centuries trade between Britain and other countries was controlled in various ways by the British government – mainly through the imposition of import and export duties on goods entering and leaving the country. The main purpose of these duties was to raise revenue (i.e. money) for the government. They were also intended in some cases to protect British producers from foreign competition. During the first half of the 19th century the levying of these duties came under increasing attack from those who felt that Britain would benefit economically from a system of free trade. The first assignment (9.1) in this chapter looks at some of the arguments for and against free trade that were used at the time. It concentrates on the Corn Laws, the import duties that always caused the greatest controversy.

From the mid-19th century until the 1920s Britain was a free trade country, with virtually no restrictions on the import and export of goods. Despite demands from time to time for a return to protectionism – especially in the early years of the 20th century – free trade seemed to benefit Britain. Production and trade rose rapidly for much of the period, though with increasing competition from other countries from the last quarter of the 19th century onwards. The worldwide economic depression of the inter-war years led eventually to the reintroduction of import controls, as a way of protecting Britain's industries from foreign competition. Import controls of one kind or another have persisted ever since.

After the Second World War some European countries came to see that there were advantages in the formation of trading associations. Members of these associations would agree to reduce duties on the import of each other's goods. Until the 1960s Britain stayed aloof from the most important of these associations, the EEC, convinced that its economic links with the former British empire were more important than those with Europe. The second assignment (9.2) looks at the way in which British views changed and at the steps that were eventually taken to bring Britain into the EEC. Britain's entry into the European Community in 1972 was one of the most important turning points in British history. We are still living through its consequences today.

Assignment 9.1
The debate over the Corn Laws

There had been controversy about the Corn Laws long before the formation of the Anti-Corn Law League in 1838. The League, however, was very effective in concentrating public attention on the question. The debate was particularly intense in the first half of the 1840s, dividing both middle-class and upper-class opinion and, at the time when the Corn Laws were actually repealed in 1846, splitting the Conservative Party into two factions. This assignment examines the arguments that were used for and against repeal. It also looks at the motives that influenced Peel to pass this measure.

Source A

From a petition to the House of Commons sent in 1841 at a time when the government was considering an alteration to the sliding scale. The sliding scale was a scale of duties imposed on the import of foreign corn. It allowed the import duty to be adjusted up and down to reflect the price of British corn, i.e. as the price of British corn went down so import duties rose. The 'proposed alteration' referred to in the source was intended to allow foreign corn to enter the country more easily.

> The humble petition of the undersigned, the Inhabitants of North and South Cadbury, in the county of Somerset, Sheweth, ... the proposed alteration of the present Corn Law will be, if carried into effect, attended with dangerous consequences to the Nation, deluding the people with the expectation that cheap bread could be obtained without a corresponding lowering of wages ... we consider it the first duty of the **legislature** to ensure ... a certain, regular and efficient supply of wheat for the consumption of the people ... every security and encouragement must be afforded to home cultivation: ... it will be most ruinous ... to place dependence upon foreign countries for the supply of wheat, instead of mainly relying on our native resources ...
>
> **legislature:** parliament

Source B

From a speech by Richard Cobden, leader of the Anti-Corn Law League, given on 3 July 1844

In the first place, we want free trade in corn, because we think it just; ... We do not seek free trade in corn primarily for the purpose of purchasing it at a cheaper money rate; we require it at the natural price of the world's market, whether it becomes dearer ... or whether it is cheaper, it matters not to us, provided the people of this country have it at its natural price, and every source of supply is freely opened ...

Source C

From a speech by Richard Cobden

To pay for that corn, more manufactures would be required from this country; this would lead to an increased demand for labour in the manufacturing districts, which would necessarily be attended with a rise in wages, in order that the goods might be made for the purpose of exchanging for the corn brought from abroad... I observe there are narrow-minded men in the agricultural districts, telling us, "Oh, if you allow Free Trade, and bring in a quarter of corn from abroad, it is quite clear that you will sell one quarter less in England" ... What! I would ask, if you set more people to work at better wages – if you can clear your streets of those spectres which are now haunting your thoroughfares begging their daily bread – if you can depopulate your workhouses and clear off the two million of paupers which now exist in the land, and put them to work at productive industry – do you not think that they would consume some of the wheat as well as you; and may not they be as we are now, consumers of wheaten bread by millions, instead of existing on their present miserable **dietary?**

dietary: diet

Source D

From a speech by Richard Cobden in the House of Commons, 25 August 1841. Cobden describes a conference of 650 ministers held that year in Manchester.

There were at that meeting members of the established church, of the Church of Rome, Independents, Baptists, members of the Church of Scotland, and of the Secession Church, Methodists, and, indeed, ministers of every other denomination ... Those revered Gentlemen had prepared and signed a petition, in which they prayed for the removal of **those laws** – laws which, they stated, **violated the Scriptures** ... and he (Cobden) would remind honourable Gentlemen that, besides these 650 ministers, there were 1,500 others, from whom letters had been received, offering up their prayers in their several localities to incline the will of Him who ruled princes and **potentates** to turn your hearts to justice and mercy.

those laws: the Corn Laws
violated the Scriptures: were against the teachings of the Bible
potentates: rulers

Source E

From a letter to Peel from Henry Goulburn, Peel's Chancellor of the Exchequer, written in 1845

...In my opinion the party of which you are the head is the only barrier which remains against the revolutionary effects of the Reform Bill. So long as that party remains unbroken, whether in or out of power, it has the means of doing much good, or at least of preventing much evil. But if it be broken in pieces by a destruction of confidence in its leaders (and I cannot but think that an abandonment of the Corn Law would produce that result), I see nothing before us but the ... ultimate triumph of unrestrained democracy.

Source F

From an open letter to the Electors of the City of London, issued by Lord John Russell, the Whig leader, on 22 November 1845. This letter was written in Edinburgh and is usually known as the Edinburgh Letter.

... But I confess that in the general subject my views have in the course of twenty years undergone a great alteration. I used to be of the opinion that corn was an exception to the general rules of political economy; but observation and experience have convinced me that we ought to abstain from all interference with the supply of food ...

Let us, then, unite to put an end to a system which has been proved to be the blight of commerce, the ***bane*** *of agriculture, the source of bitter divisions among classes, the causes of* ***penury****, fever,* ***mortality****, and crime among the people ...*

bane: something that causes harm
penury: poverty
mortality: death

Source G

From a speech in the House of Commons by Sir Robert Peel, 15 May 1846

... Sir, I do not rest my support of this Bill merely on the temporary ground of scarcity in Ireland ... but I believe that scarcity left no alternative to us but to undertake the consideration of this question ... I think that a permanent adjustment of the question is not only imperative, but the best policy for all concerned ... we wish to elevate in ... society that great class which gains its support by manual labour ...The mere interests of the landlords – ... important as they are, are subordinate to the great question – what is calculated to increase the comforts, to improve the condition, ... of the millions who subsist by manual labour, whether they are engaged in manufactures or in agriculture? I wish to convince them that our object has been so to **apportion taxation**, ... and transfer it, so far as is consistent with the public good, to those who are better enabled to bear it.

apportion taxation: decide how much tax different groups of people will have to pay

Activities

1 Which of Sources A to G supported the Corn Laws? Which of Sources A to G opposed the Corn Laws? In the case of each source, quote one phrase or sentence which shows that the author of the source either supported or opposed the Corn Laws.

2 Study the sources which opposed the Corn Laws. In the case of each of these sources identify, in your own words, the arguments used in that source to support the repeal of the Corn Laws. Organise your answer like this:

Source B

Argument (1): it is wrong to interfere with the 'natural price' of any item of trade

Argument (2): it will not harm farm labourers because there will be more jobs open to them after repeal

Argument (3): landowners will not be financially worse off, especially if they try to farm more productively

etc.

3 Study the list of arguments you have identified in answer to Question 2. Where a number of arguments are used in one source, comment on which of these (if any) you think would have been most important to the author of the source.

4 How similar were the arguments used by the various sources that are opposed to the Corn Laws? Refer to the sources in support of your answer.

5 Study the sources that supported the Corn Laws. Describe in your own words the arguments used in these sources.

6 Why did Peel decide to repeal the Corn Laws in 1846? Refer both to Source G and to your background knowledge.

Assignment 9.2
Britain applies to join the EEC

This assignment has two main purposes. The first is to help you explore Britain's ambivalent attitude towards the European Economic Community during the early years of its existence ('ambivalent' means having differing views about something – in this case whether or not Britain would benefit from joining the Community). The second is to encourage you to evaluate particular kinds of evidence, and especially in this case oral evidence spoken long after the event. The sources all refer to Britain's application to join the EEC in 1962 – 3. The written sources are all taken from *The Price of Victory* by Michael Charlton, first published in 1983. The politicians and civil servants quoted in this book were interviewed in 1980 as part of a series of programmes broadcast on BBC Radio 3.

Source A
A Vicky cartoon published in 1962 in the *Evening Standard*. The cartoon imitates the Bayeux Tapestry's account of the Norman conquest of 1066. The three figures on the right of the first box in the cartoon represent (from left to right): Harold Macmillan, Prime Minister; R. A. Butler, Deputy Prime Minister; and Edward Heath, at that time a Foreign Office minister.

Source B
A Vicky cartoon, published in the *New Statesman* in 1962. The figure on the left represents Harold Macmillan. The Rome Treaty was the treaty in 1957 that had set up the EEC. The wolf is the Roman wolf from the story of Romulus and Remus.

Source C

From an interview with Sir Herbert Andrew, a Board of Trade official who was part of the UK delegation during the negotiations of 1961–3

Looking back, it seems rather absurd but, when we tried EFTA (the European Free Trade Area) with the non-members of the Community, we had the idea that it was a kind of negotiating contest. Many people did not believe that the Community would hold together. We were still, I think, influenced by the immediate past. While we'd had a good many hopeful moves in the years after the war, we had seen a number of policies fail, but we hadn't realised really that the *reason* they failed was because of our own relatively declining strength.

Source D

From an interview with R. A. Butler, Deputy Prime Minister at the time of the negotiations

At Marlborough House we got together the whole Commonwealth, and before it took place we had terrible talks with Bob Menzies, the Australian Prime Minister. Bob Menzies thought that we were traitors, and New Zealand did too. New Zealand did because of butter and sheep, you see, but Australia did on broader grounds of policy. Bob, as you know, was half a British statesman really. He was always coming over here! And he was dead against it. He gave great hell, you know, to Harold, and partly to me, and we decided it wasn't much worth going on. But then we persuaded Bob that, on the lines I have been talking to you, our Empire was gone, and a lot of our strength was gone, and had we not better join an economic unit where we could be a competitor with the USA and the USSR? And that was the final argument that appealed to Bob ... But it was a very close thing up until the end.

Source E

From the diary of Harold Macmillan, January 1963

... the great question remains, "What is the alternative?" to the European Community. If we are honest, we must say there is none – had there been the chance of a Commonwealth Free Trade Area we should have grasped it long ago.

Source F

From an interview with R. A. Butler

We saw the Prince of Wales say the other day that Britain is not a first-class power. I wish somebody had stopped him. He oughtn't to say things like that. But the fact is that it's partially true, you see, and we have changed incredibly from what we were. Especially, of course, in naval power and the control of the seas ...

Activities

1 Using your own knowledge, describe what happened to Britain's application to join the EEC in 1961–3.

2 Study Sources A and B.

(i) Tell the story of each of these cartoons in your own words.

(ii) What was the cartoonist's attitude towards these events?

(iii) Are Sources A and B of any interest to the historian?

3 What do you learn from Sources C, D, E and F about reasons why the British government had been reluctant to join the EEC?

4 What do you learn from Sources C, D, E and F about reasons why the British government decided in 1961 to apply for membership of the EEC?

5 Sources C, D and F are all examples of oral evidence. What do you think are the strengths and weaknesses of this type of evidence, as revealed in these sources?

Further activities

1 (i) Using a blank map of the world, identify *three* areas or countries to which Britain exported large quantities of goods in the 19th century. Describe the nature of this export trade and explain its importance for Britain.

(ii) Using the same map, identify *three different* areas from which Britain imported large quantities of goods in the 19th century. Describe the nature of this import trade and explain its importance for Britain.

2 What was the importance *of three* of the following in the development of Britain's overseas trade during the 19th century: steamships; refrigeration; railways; port improvements; the telegraph; emigration?

3 Compare figures for Britain's overseas trade today with figures for any period before the 1970s. What differences do you notice and how would you explain them?

10 *Living and Working Conditions*
to 1870

Look at the pictures in this chapter (Source A of Assignment 10.1 and Source F of Assignment 10.2). It is scenes such as these that spring to mind when most of us think about working and living conditions in 19th century Britain. These are the sorts of scenes that we associate particularly with the *19th* century. Such conditions were not, however, new. There had always been a high death rate. People had often lived in great squalor. Children had frequently worked from an early age. None of these social problems first appeared with the industrial revolution.

What *was* new in the 19th century was the scale of the problem. The rapid growth in population, industry, and towns meant that old problems were now much more visible. In the past people had usually just ignored them. With the industrial revolution it was difficult to pretend that they did not exist. As a result, the 19th century saw a growing demand for reform. In particular more and more people came to feel that it was the *government's* responsibility to put these conditions right. This in itself was something new.

The assignments in this chapter are concerned with two of the most important of these social problems: conditions in the mines (Assignment 10.1) and public health in towns (Assignment 10.2). Assignment 10.1 concentrates on the attitudes and feelings of the workers themselves. Assignment 10.2 looks mainly at what governments and middle-class people felt ought to be done to improve these conditions.

Assignment 10.1
Child labour in the coal mines

The industrial revolution and the growth in Britain's population led to a huge increase in the demand for coal. Coal was needed for steam engines and for many other purposes in industry, as well as for the railways and for use in the home. It was also one of Britain's major exports. The country produced more coal than the rest of the world put together. As a result more and more people were employed in coal mining. Women and children had always worked in the mines, but in the early 19th century their numbers increased.

During the 1830s there was growing pressure on the government to introduce restrictions on the employment of children in factories. This factory reform movement attracted a great deal of support. People became involved in this movement for many different reasons. Some were simply horrified at the appalling physical conditions. Others were shocked by the ignorance and immorality of working-class communities. Their concern was to put women back where they were supposed to belong – in the home – as well as to make sure that children received proper instruction, especially in morals and religion. Some working-class people supported the movement mainly in the hope that restrictions on women and children would lead to better conditions for male workers.

As a result of the movement for factory reform, there was also a growing demand for the regulation of conditions in mines. During the 1830s and 1840s a number of committees and Royal Commissions were set up to investigate conditions in both factories and mines. One of the most important was the Children's Employment Commission whose reports led to the Mines Act of 1842 and the Factory Act of 1844. Most of the sources you will be studying in this assignment are extracts from this Commission's report on mines, published in 1842. This was the first government report on working conditions to include illustrations, some of which are shown on this page.

The purpose of the assignment is to look at the attitudes and feelings of the people involved, especially those of the miners themselves.

Source A
Illustrations from the *Report of the Children's Employment Commission (Mines)*, 1842

Source B

From the Report of the Children's Employment Commission (Mines), 1842

When a child first goes into the pits (in North Wales) he is taken down by his father, or some friend who has employment in the work; he is usually put to keep an air-door, or to some light work. In examining the boys, few would own that they felt much fear or distress on entering the pits, and all say they very soon became used and reconciled to their work. They are for the most part children of **colliers,** and from infancy familiar with the idea of under-ground work, and anxious to go below and begin to work.

This wish of course meets with no opposition from their parents, who, lured by the wages, are never backward in sending their children to the pits as soon as they can get them into employ(ment), so that no sooner is a collier's son able to exert a little muscular force than he becomes an under-ground machine, **destitute of the slightest mental cultivation.**

colliers: workers in the coal mines or collieries
destitute of the slightest mental cultivation: with hardly any mind at all

Source C

From the Report of the Children's Employment Commission (Mines), 1842

Susan Pitchforth, aged 11, living at Elland:
I have worked at this pit going two years ... I run 24 **corves** a day; I cannot come up till I have done them all ... My father slaps me sometimes upon the head, or upon the back, so as to make me cry ...

A very ignorant child (commented Mr Scriven, the Sub-Commissioner). She stood shivering before me from cold. The rag that hung about her waist was once **a shift**, which is as black as the coal she thrusts, and saturated with water, from the dripping of the roof and shaft. During my examination of her the banksman whom I had left in the pit came to the public-house and wanted to take her away, because, as he expressed himself, it was not decent that she should be (her person) exposed to us; oh no! it was criminal above ground; and, like the two or three other colliers in the cabin, he became evidently mortified that these deeds of darkness should be brought to light.

corves: carriages in which the coal is transported
shift: simple dress

Source D

From the Report of the Children's Employment Commission (Mines), 1842

Sarah Gooder, age 8:
I'm a **trapper** in the Gawber pit. It does not tire me, but I have to trap without a light, and I'm scared. Sometimes I sing when I have a light, but not in the dark; I dare not sing then . . . I would like to be at school far better than in the pit.

trapper: someone who opens and closes the air doors inside the mines. These doors were essential in order to keep the mines properly ventilated.

Source E

From J.R. Leifchild, *Our Coal Fields and Our Coal Pits,* 1853

The trappers are stationary, and if found away from their doors are thumped and threatened ... Many sit there, too, in fear of the **hobgoblins** to be met with in the pit; and the reputation of hobgoblins is sustained for their good behaviour.

hobgoblins: wicked gnomes

Source F

From *Hansard, House of Lords Debates, 24 June 1842*

The Marquess of Londonderry, presenting a petition to the House of Lords from owners of collieries in Durham and Northumberland, said that it appeared that the Commissioners had come to this inquiry fresh from the Factory Commission, with all the prejudices and desire of finding similar oppressions amongst the miners to those which they had found amongst the manufacturing population. Their instructions were to examine the children themselves, and the mode in which they collected their evidence – communicating with artful boys and ignorant young girls, and putting questions in a manner which in many cases seemed to suggest an answer, was anything but ... fair ... Again he thought the manner in which the Report had been accompanied by pictures of an extravagant and disgusting, and in some cases of a scandalous and obscene character, was not such as should have been adopted in a **grave** publication, and was more calculated to excite the feelings than to enlighten the judgment ...

(The document presented to the House by his Lordship contained the following): The trapper's employment is neither cheerless, dull, nor stupefying; nor is he, nor can he be, kept in solitude and darkness all the time he is in the pit ...The trapper is generally cheerful and contented, and to be found, like other children of his age, occupied with some childish amusement – as cutting sticks, making models of windmills, waggons, etc., and frequently in drawing figures with chalk on the door, modelling figures of men and animals in clay, etc.

grave: serious

Activities

1 What do you learn from Sources A, B, C and D about the methods used by the Children's Employment Commission when investigating conditions in coal mines?

2 Do you think the report of this commission is likely to be a reliable source of evidence for conditions in coal mines? Explain your answer, referring to Sources A, B, C, D and F where appropriate.

3 What do you learn from Sources A, B, C and D about the jobs given to children in the coal mines?

4 Do Sources A, B, C, D and E show that children employed in mines hated their work? Refer in detail to the sources in support of your answer.

5 'Parents and adult coal miners do not seem to have been opposed to the employment of children in the mines.' Do Sources A, B, C, D and E support this statement? Give reasons for your answer.

6 Study Source F.
(i) Is there anything to be said for the Marquess of Londonderry's criticism of the use of pictures in the *Report of the Children's Employment Commission?*

(ii) The petition by the mine owners gives a very different account of the life of a trapper from the one in the report. Is this a simple case of mine owners telling deliberate lies? Explain your answer.

Assignment 10.2

Why was public health such an important issue in mid-19th century Britain?

Although it is hard to believe, Source F shows a back street in Glasgow *after* the introduction of a number of important sanitary improvements. It is difficult for us to conceive of conditions that are worse than these. It therefore takes quite an effort to imagine how, to contemporaries, such conditions might actually have seemed an improvement on what had gone before.

Trying to understand how people in the past thought and felt is one of the main tasks facing anyone studying history. The purpose of this assignment is to help you to understand how people at the time thought about public health. It isn't good enough just to think how *you* would have responded – because you are not a Victorian and many of the things that you take for granted would not have been taken for granted 150 years ago. For example, it is often assumed that the only reason for supporting sanitary reform was to stop people from suffering unnecessarily. As Sources A and B suggest, it wasn't as simple as such an explanation suggests.

Most of the sources for this assignment date from the 1840s and 1850s. This was a period of great interest in public health, with growing concern about the epidemic diseases and high death rates that were prevalent in many of Britain's towns. Source A is an extract from Edwin Chadwick's influential *Sanitary Report*, published in 1842. This report recommended major changes in drainage and sewage together with stronger powers for government in order to ensure that improvements were actually carried out.

Chadwick's report led to the passing of the Public Health Act of 1848, which set up a General Board of Health but gave it few powers to compel local authorities to carry out reforms. Opposition to Chadwick, as well as to the whole idea of central government interference, was such that the General Board was disbanded in 1854. Sanitary reform, however, did not cease and later in the century legislation finally gave government most of the powers that Chadwick had recommended. In time – though often very slowly – conditions in towns began to improve. More slowly still, death rates began to fall.

Source A

From a preface to a new edition of his novel *Oliver Twist* by Charles Dickens, written in 1851. Dickens was an active supporter of sanitary reform.

> I have always been convinced that this Reform (slum clearance) must precede all other Social Reforms; that it must prepare the way for Education, even for Religion; and that, without it, those classes of the people which increase the fastest, must become so desperate and be made so miserable, as to bear within themselves the certain seeds of ruin to the whole community.

Source B

Extracts from the 'main conclusions' of Chadwick's *Report on the Sanitary Condition of the Labouring Population* ,1842

... That the annual loss of life from filth and bad ventilation is greater than the loss from death and wounds in any wars in which the country has been engaged in modern times.

That of the 43,000 cases of widowhood, and 112,000 cases of destitute orphanage relieved from the poor's rates in England and Wales alone, it appears that the greatest proportion of deaths of the heads of families occurred from the above specified and other removable causes; that their ages were under 45 years ...

That the population so exposed is less susceptible of moral influences, and the effects of education are more **transient** than with a healthy population.

That these adverse circumstances tend to produce an adult population short-lived, **improvident,** reckless, and **intemperate**, and with **habitual avidity for sensual gratification**.

That these habits lead to the abandonment of all the conveniences and decencies of life, and especially lead to the overcrowding of their homes, which is destructive to the morality as well as the health of large classes of both sexes.

That defective town cleansing fosters habits of the most abject degradation and tends to the demoralisation of large numbers of human beings, who subsist by means of what they find amidst the noxious filth accumulated in neglected streets and bye-places.

That the expenses of local public works are in general unequally and unfairly assessed, oppressively and uneconomically collected, by separate collections, wastefully expended in separate and inefficient operations by unskilled and practically irresponsible officers.

transient: short-lived
improvident: making no provision/careless
intemperate: drunken
habitual avidity for sensual gratification: always seeking the pleasures of the senses

Source C

From *Bleak House*, a novel by Charles Dickens, published in 1852–3. 'Tom-all-Alone's' is a London slum street in which one of the characters in the novel lives.

It is a black, dilapidated street, avoided by all decent people; where the crazy houses were seized upon, when their decay was far advanced, by some bold vagrants, who, after establishing their own possession, took to letting them out in lodgings. Now, these tumbling tenements contain, by night, a swarm of misery ... these ruined shelters have bred a crowd of foul existence that crawls in and out of gaps in walls and boards; and coils itself to sleep ... where the rain drips in; and comes and goes, fetching and carrying fever, and sowing more evil in its every footprint ... Twice lately there has been a crash and a cloud of dust ... and each time, a house has fallen.

Source D

An extract from the *Report on the Sanitary Condition of the City of London*, compiled by John Simon, Medical Officer of Health, in 1850

There are constructional defects of houses and courts whereby their crowded inhabitants are excluded from a sufficiency of light and air, and constrained, without remission or change, to breathe an atmosphere **foetid** with their own stagnant **exhalations** ... It is an incontrovertible fact that **subsistence** in the courts is an unhealthy and shortlived subsistence in comparison with that of dwellers in the open street ...

courts: courtyards/narrow streets without an exit at the other end
foetid: stinking
exhalations: breath/body odours
subsistence: life

Source E

From Friedrich Engels, *The Condition of the Working Class in England*, 1844-5. Engels was a German resident in Britain and one of the most important socialist thinkers of the 19th century. This passage refers to Manchester.

> Right and left a multitude of covered passages led from the main street into numerous courts, and he who turns in thither gets into a filth and disgusting grime, the equal of which is not to be found – especially in the courts which lead down to the (River) Irk, and which contain unqualifiedly the most horrible dwellings which I have yet beheld. In one of these courts there stands directly at the entrance, at the end of the covered passage, a privy without a door, so dirty that the inhabitants can pass into and out of the court only by passing through foul pools of stagnant urine and excrement.

Source F

A back street in Glasgow, 1868

Activities

1 Study Source F carefully. List at least *four* features shown in the photograph which illustrate improvements in public health taking place in the mid-19th century.

2 (i) Study Source B. Why does Chadwick think that sanitary reform is important? Read Source B carefully, noting down as many reasons as you can find and then using your notes to help you plan an answer to this question.

(ii) Study Source A. Why does Dickens think that slum clearance is important? Answer in your own words.

(iii) Referring to Sources A, B and C, say whether or not you think Chadwick and Dickens agreed about public health.

3 Dickens' novels have sometimes been criticised for the way in which they exaggerate and sensationalise conditions in British towns. Do these sources support this criticism? Explain your answer with reference to all these sources.

4 Give reasons why members of *three* of the following groups of people were often opposed to public health reform in the mid-19th century: middle-class ratepayers; those with shares in water companies; Improvement Commissioners; slaughterhouse owners; slum landlords; local councillors.

Further activities

1 Organise a class debate on the 1833 Factory Bill, using the arguments that would have been used by supporters and opponents at the time. After the debate, make a table listing the main arguments on both sides. Then write a short commentary explaining what the various arguments suggest about the motives and feelings of those who used them.

2 Make notes on the terms of the Factory Acts of 1802 (Health and Morals of Apprentices Act), 1833, 1844, 1847 and 1853. What were (a) the main similarities and (b) the main differences between *two* of these acts?

3 Who gained and who lost as a result of the passing of the Factory Acts of 1833 and 1844 and the Mines Act of 1842? Explain your anwer.

4 Look carefully at plans and photographs of 19th century water closets (toilets). What do you learn from these about the attitudes and way of life of people in 19th century Britain?

5 Find out about drainage and sewage disposal in your own area today. What similarities and differences do you notice between provision now and provision in the first half of the 19th century?

11 *Living and Working Conditions* *from 1870*

During the last 150 years British people have become very much more prosperous. Over this period there has been a huge rise in average real wages (a 'real wage' is what you are able to buy with the money you earn). Average real wages were considerably higher in 1900 than they had been in 1850. Despite the economic problems of the inter-war years, they continued to rise over the first half of the 20th century. After 1945 they rose much more dramatically.

By the late 20th century ordinary people were living in conditions that, in many cases, would have been beyond the wildest dreams of their great-grandparents. As well as having more money to spend, people lived much longer, were in better health, were better housed, and were protected by insurance against some of the effects of sickness, unemployment and old age. Labour-saving devices had also freed them from the worst drudgery of domestic chores.

No-one would disagree that this is what has happened. And yet in many ways this picture of ever-increasing prosperity is misleading. It is misleading because it just looks at what has happened on average over a long period of time. It distracts attention from all those groups of people or parts of the country that did not share in the overall prosperity. It ignores the many variations in the pattern – the years when living standards fell rather than rose; the people unable to find employment at a time when employed workers were prospering; the way in which prosperity and poverty could come and go even within the life of one individual.

Once you begin to study particular groups of people, particular parts of the country, and even particular individuals, the whole pattern becomes much more complex. During the late 19th century, for example, the living standards of Yorkshire textile workers were much higher than those of Dorset farm labourers. In the 1930s (and again in the 1980s) high levels of unemployment prevented many people from sharing in the growth of prosperity. Throughout the whole period male workers have been far better off than female workers. Huge differences between regions and groups of workers exist to the present day. In recent years they have become even more noticeable.

The assignments in this chapter are intended to help you to explore some of these differences within British society. The first assignment (11.1) looks at the lives of a small number of individuals at the end of the 19th century and the beginning of the 20th century. It tries to show you how one person's experiences could be very different from another's, even when the two people belonged to the same social group. The second assignment (11.2) looks at the differences between the north and the south and at how these differences have influenced life in Britain throughout the period you are studying.

Assignment 11.1
Memories of childhood in the late 19th and early 20th centuries

The sources for this assignment are all autobiographies, either written or spoken. An *autobiography* is a person's account of his or her own life. All the sources describe childhood in England at the end of the 19th and the beginning of the 20th centuries. They were all written or spoken long after the events they describe. The assignment has two purposes: (i) to help you to find out about living conditions during the period; and (ii) to examine the strengths and weaknesses of a particular type of historical evidence.

Source A
From the unpublished autobiography of Faith Osgerby. The writer was born in Beverley, East Yorkshire, the third of a family of seven children. Her father was a stonemason who also kept cows for a milk-round.

I have now passed my seventieth birthday, being born in 1890, and I think I will call this "My Memoirs" as my "Life Story" would I fear not be pleasant reading all the time. Some of it too would be distressing to me to write... People tell me I have a good memory, so I shall try to remember episodes in my young life which seemed to impress me at the time, and write them down as I remember them ...

When I was three years old we moved into Eastgate, just before my brother George was born. Babies were not welcomed in our family. I have heard my mother say on more than one occasion in her middle age that if she had to live her life again and knew as much as she did then she wouldn't have had one of us. She told me she even took gunpowder to get rid of *me*, mixing it to a paste in a soapdish on her washstand every night. I hope she didn't hold it against me that I refused to budge ...

All my life has been ruled by fear I think. It must have been the first emotion I ever felt, fear of swift punishment. I seem to be painting an awful picture of my mother. I don't really mean to do that because I do realise she must have had a great deal to put up with all the time. Seven children to clothe and feed and little enough money to do it. Also my elder sister being an invalid from infancy (with polio) must have been a very great trouble to her. Doctors had to be paid for their services, and I am quite sure my sister had everyhting done for her that could be done in those days. I remember two doctors coming to the house to operate on her legs and feet.

Source B

From the unpublished autobiography of Jack Lanigan. The writer was born in Salford, Lancashire, in 1890. His father, a skilled worker, died while he and his brother were very young.

"Ave yer any bread left, master?"

That was the theme song of hundreds of youngsters of whom my brother Matt and I could be counted. We had our pitches for begging. I, along with two other hungry kids, stood outside the gates of Mather & Platt, Ltd, then situated off Bury Street, Salford, waiting for the gates to open at 6 p.m. When they did, the workers would file out into the street carrying their wicker lunch baskets and when they heard our voices, "Ave yer any bread left master?" they would hand anything they had left out to us. When I had got sufficient for my mother and brother, I made tracks for home and these left-overs would be shared with a cup of tea; if no tea then with a cup of water. We drank more water than tea even if the latter was only one shilling a pound.

The days of 1890–1900 were tough, they were days that were not easily cast aside. One cannot go to bed hungry and get up in the morning with that same feeling without leaving a scar on the memory ...

Besides the heartbreaking cry, "Ave yer any bread left master?" there was another common cry at all the "Fish and Chip" shops, "Can you spare any scrapings, Sir?" Believe me this was no joke. The kids, myself included, travelled from shop to shop to ensure we had collected sufficient for the family; we became regular customers as one would say. These scrapings with some bread made a meal.

We lived at No. 1 Thomas Street, off Brewery Street, Salford (since demolished), two up and one down, no back yard, because it was back-to-back with a large **six-seated privy midden** – it was known as a communal midden. The back bedroom, where Matt and I slept, was immediately over this bedroom midden, the bedroom floor also acted as ceiling to this obnoxious structure. The smell in our bedroom was vile ... There was very little sleep at weekends on account of the drunks and free-for-all scraps. I cannot remember having any bedding on our bed. The coverings to cover our little bodies were old coats and sacks ... If ever I was invited to the house of a playmate, their beds were similar.

six-seated privy midden: the dung heap (midden) from a six-seater lavatory. These lavatories were shared by a number of houses.

Source C

From the unpublished autobiography of Alice Foley. The writer was born in Bolton, Lancashire, in 1891, the sixth child in her family. Her father drank heavily and was often out of work.

Each Monday morning, after brushing and sorting out the Sunday clothes, such as they were, a big parcel was made up; mother carried this whilst I, clutching her skirt, trotted along quite joyfully. Walking quickly down the back street we nipped smartly in at the side door of the "Golden Balls" at the corner of Punch Street. The pawnshop was owned by a big, jovial man who I later knew as "Bill". He was invariably perched on a high stool behind a long wire-netted counter. As mother was a regular customer he never opened her parcel, but placed it in one of the cubicles just above his head, and then slipped some silver coins to her under the grill ...

We were brought up mainly out of (my mother's) wash-tub earnings. Frequently I accompanied her to various better-off houses, and sitting on the floor amongst a pile of dirty clothes played games and prattled aloud whilst she silently scrubbbed shirts or mangled heavy sheets ...

When father was recovering from a boozing bout, his temper was most vicious and unpredictable. I recall his following mother persistently round the kitchen whining monotonously, "Lend us a penny, Meg, lend us a penny; I'm choking." At length, in a fit of desperation, a penny was flung on to the table, whilst mother snatched up her shawl and vanished into the street to find temporary refuge in a neighbour's home.

It was then my job to fetch a gill of beer from the nearby "White Hart" ... On arriving home with a jug of flat beer, I was greeted with "Where the hell have you been?" and a volley of oaths. Sometimes I dodged out of the back door, but more frequently mooned around ... in the hope of coaxing father to go to bed and so leave the family in peace.

Source D

From an interview with Mrs E. Sillar for BBC Radio. The speaker is referring to her childhood in England at the beginning of the 20th century. The date of the interview is not known.

> There was, I suppose, a great deal of poverty. Naturally, I didn't know much about that as a child. My own dear nurse and the two faithful maids who served us – they never complained of poverty, and when they retired, they were comfortable and had nice places to live, and were always nicely dressed, and could go off for little holidays. It's difficult to know what poverty is.

Activities

1 Read Sources A, B and C. Use the table below to help you record what you learn from these sources about living conditions at the end of the 19th century and the beginning of the 20th century.

	Source A	Source B	Source C
Family size			
Health/medical care			
Diet			
Housing			
Sanitation			
Employment			
Any particular reasons why this family was poor			

2 (i) Using the table, describe the main differences in the ways of life of the three families referred to in Sources A, B and C.

(ii) What reasons help to explain these differences?

(iii) Did any of the three writers have a happy childhood? Explain your answer.

3 (i) Do you think the authors of Sources A, B and C described their childhood exactly as it happened? Give reasons for your answer, referring in detail to the sources.

(ii) Is any one of these three sources more valuable than the others to someone studying living conditions at the end of the 19th century? Give reasons for your answer.

4 Is Source D of any value to someone studying English social history in the early 20th century? Explain your answer.

5 Compare what you have learnt from Sources A, B, C and D with what you know about English society today. In what ways has English society changed and for what reasons?

Assignment 11.2
North and south

People sometimes ask about 'the British sense of identity' – in other words what it means to be British, as distinct, for example, from being French or Canadian. This is a difficult question to answer, partly because it is the kind of thing we take for granted. It is also difficult because within Britain there are many different identities. Britain, first of all, consists of a number of formerly independent countries: England, Wales and Scotland (with Northern Ireland also forming part of the United Kingdom). Each of these, to a varying extent, still has a strong sense of being different from the rest of Britain. This is particularly true in the case of Scotland, with its separate legal and educational systems, its own established church, and its distinctive customs. Even within England, however, people have often had a more limited sense of identity that was just as strong as their sense of being 'British' or 'English'. People were 'working class' or 'Londoners' or 'Lancastrians' first and only 'English' or 'British' second.

This assignment looks at one way in which England has sometimes seemed to be divided: between the north and the south. This is a division that has been talked about for a very long time. In many ways of course it is a very artificial division. The differences between the various parts of 'the north' or 'the south' often seem far greater than anything these areas have in common. It is impossible, however, to ignore the fact that England has developed in many different ways and that some of the main differences have been between areas mostly in 'the north' and areas mostly in 'the south'. The purpose of the assignment is to help you look at how people have experienced this north/south divide at different times. It is also designed to help you make sense of what is still a very important feature of British life at the end of the 20th century.

Source A

From the novel *North and South* by Mrs Elizabeth Gaskell, published in 1855. The episode in this extract takes place in a northern town. The three characters are Nicholas, a northern working man, Bessy, his daughter, and Margaret, a young woman from the south of England who has recently arrived in the north.

At last he (Nicholas) said:

"I know nought of your ways down South. I have heerd they're a pack of spiritless, down-trodden men; welly **clemmed** to death; too much dazed wi' clemming to know when they're put upon. Now, it's not so here. We know when we're put upon, and we'en too much blood in us to stand it. We just take our hands fro' our looms, and say, 'Yo' may clem us. but yo'll not put upon us, my masters!' And be danged to 'em, they shan't this time!"

"I wish I lived down South," said Bessy.

"There's a deal to bear there," said Margaret. "There are sorrows to bear everywhere. There is very hard bodily labour to be gone through, with very little food to give strength."

"But it's out of doors," sais Bessy. "And away from the endless, endless noise, and sickening heat."

"It's sometimes in heavy rain, and sometimes in bitter cold. A young person can stand it; but an old man gets racked with rheumatism, and bent and withered before his time; yet he must just work on the same, or else go to the workhouse."

"I thought yo' were so taken wi' the ways of the South country."

"So I am," said Margaret, smiling a little, as she found herself thus caught. "I only mean, Bessy, there's good and bad in everything in this world; and as you felt the bad up here, I thought it was but fair you should know the bad down there."

"And yo' say they never strike down there?" asked Nicholas, abruptly.

"No!" said Margaret; "I think they have too much sense."

"An' I think," replied he, dashing the ashes out of his pipe with so much vehemence that it broke, "it's not that they've too much sense, but that they've too little spirit."

clemmed: starved

Source B

From a book published in 1934 by the English writer J.B. Priestley. The full title of the book is *English Journey, being a rambling but truthful account of what one man saw and heard and felt and thought during a journey through England during the autumn of the year 1933.*

Southampton to Newcastle, Newcastle to Norwich: memories rose like milk coming to the boil. I had seen England. I had seen a lot of Englands. How many? At once, three disengaged themselves from the shifting mass. There was first, Old England, the country of the cathedrals and minsters and manor houses and inns, of Parson and Squire; guide-book and quaint highways and byways England ... It has long ceased to earn its own living. I am for scrupulously preserving the most enchanting bits of it, such as the cathedrals and the colleges and the Cotswolds, and for letting the rest take its chance ...

Then, I decided, there is nineteenth-century England, the industrial England of coal, iron, steel, cotton, wool, railways; of thousands of rows of little houses all alike, sham Gothic churches, square-faced chapels, Town Halls ... mills, foundries, warehouses ... back-to-back houses, detached villas with monkey-trees, Grill Rooms, railway stations, slag-heaps and "tips", dock roads, Refreshment Rooms, doss-houses, Unionist or Liberal Clubs, cindery waste ground, mill chimneys, slums, fried-fish shops, public-houses with red blinds, **bethels** in corrugated iron, good-class drapers' and confectioners' shops, a cynically devastated countryside, sooty dismal little towns, and still sootier grim fortress-like cities. This England makes up the larger part of the Midlands and the North and exists everywhere; but it is not being added to and has no new life poured into it. To the more fortunate people it was not a bad England at all, very solid and comfortable ... The less fortunate classes were very unlucky indeed in that England. They had some sort of security, which is more than many of them have now, but it was a security of monstrously long hours of work, miserable wages, and surroundings in which they lived like black-beetles at the back of a disused kitchen stove. Many of their descendants are still living in those surroundings ...

The third England, I concluded, was the new post-war England, belonging far more to the age itself than to this particular island. America, I supposed, was its real birth-place. This is the England of arterial and by-pass roads, of filling stations and factories that look like exhibition buildings, of giant cinemas and dance-halls and cafes, bungalows with tiny garages, cocktail bars, Woolworths, motor-coaches, wireless, hiking, factory girls looking like actresses, greyhound racing and dirt tracks, swimming pools, and everything given away for cigarette coupons ... It is a large-scale, mass-production job, with cut prices. You could almost accept Woolworths as its symbol ... Too much of it is simply (an) ...imitation of something not very good even in the original. There is about it a rather depressing monotony.

Source C

From *The Road to Wigan Pier* by George Orwell, published in 1937

As you travel northward your eye, accustomed to the South or East, does not notice much difference until you are beyond Birmingham. In Coventry you might as well be in Finsbury Park, and the Bull Ring in Birmingham is not unlike Norwich Market, and between all the towns of the Midlands there stretches a villa-civilization indistinguishable from that of the South. It is only when you get a little further north, to the pottery towns and beyond, that you begin to encounter the real ugliness of industrialism – an ugliness so frightful and so arresting that you are obliged, as it were, to come to terms with it ...

But when you go to the industrial North you are conscious, quite apart from the unfamiliar scenery, of entering a strange country. This is partly because of certain differences which do exist, but still more because of the North-South **antithesis** which has been rubbed into us for such a long time past. There exists in England a curious cult of Northernness, a sort of Northern snobbishness. A Yorkshireman in the South will always take care to let you know that he regards you as an inferior. If you ask him why, he will explain that it is only in the North that life is "real" life, that the industrial work done in the North is the only "real" work, that the North is inhabited by "real" people ... The Northerner has "grit", he is grim, "dour", plucky, warm-hearted, and democratic; the Southerner is snobbish, effeminate, and lazy – that at any rate is the theory ...

At the back of the mind of every Yorkshireman and every Scotchman who comes to London is a sort of Dick Whittington picture of himself as the boy who starts off by selling newspapers and ends up as Lord Mayor. And that, really, is at the bottom of his bumptiousness. But where one can make a great mistake is in imagining that this feeling extends to the genuine working class. When I first went to Yorkshire ... I expected to meet with a good deal of rudeness. But I met with nothing of the kind, and least of all among the miners.

antithesis: opposition/hostility

Activities

1 Study Source A.

(i) What do the three characters here think are the differences between north and south? Refer to the source in support of your answer.

(ii) Do you learn anything from this extract about the attitudes of the author towards north and south? Explain your answer.

2 Study Source B.

(i) Is Priestley writing in this extract about the differences between north and south? Explain your answer.

(ii) Which of Priestley's three Englands did he prefer? Give reasons for your answer.

(iii) Why does Priestley write that 'industrial England' is 'not being added to' ? Explain your answer.

(iv) Study your own local area in the 1930s. To what extent at that time was it part of 'Old England', 'industrial England' or 'the new post-war England' ?

3 Study Source C.

(i) Does Orwell think that there are any real differences between north and south? Explain your answer.

(ii) What does Orwell have to say about the attitudes of northerners? How would you explain these attitudes?

4 Do Gaskell, Priestley and Orwell share the same views about the differences between north and south? Refer to the sources in support of your answer.

Further activities

1 Interview *three* people who have memories of the period before 1945. Plan your interview so that you find out about the following: changes in real wages; changes in working conditions; diet; housing; family size. What differences do you notice between the experiences of the three people you have interviewed? How do you explain these differences?

2 In what ways have the living standards of your own family changed in the course of your own lifetime? How have these changes reflected general changes in society during this period?

3 Find out about rates of unemployment since the First World War. Why was unemployment higher at some times than at others? What have been the effects of unemployment during this period?

4 What labour-saving devices were generally available in the home (a) in 1930, (b) in 1960, and (c) in 1990? What have been the effects of the growing use of labour-saving devices in the home?

5 Watch *one* film (or part of one film) made in Britain during the period before 1960. What do you learn from this film about living or working conditions in Britain at the time at which the film was made? What are the strengths and weaknesses of this film as evidence for the social historian?

12 *Trade Unionism*
and Working-Class Movements to 1850

Look at the two front pages of early 19th century newspapers, reproduced below. Before reading on, try to work out what they illustrate...

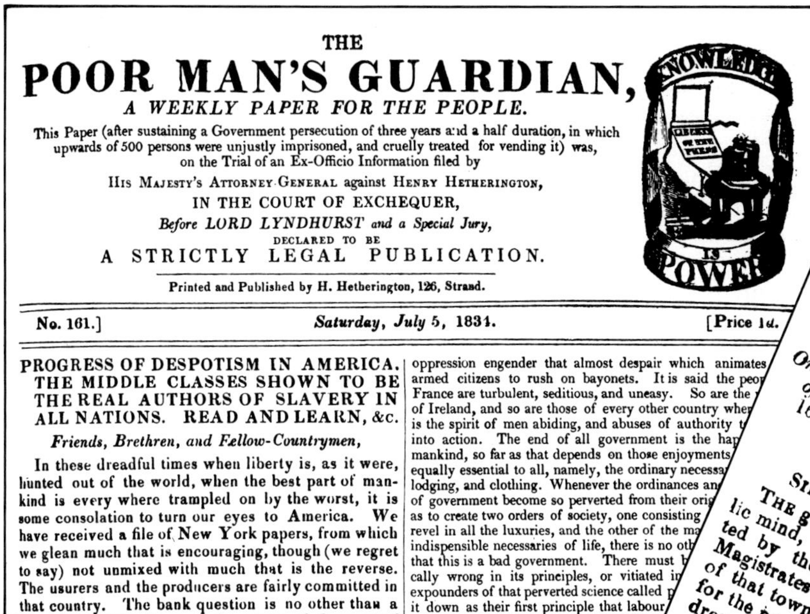

THE

POOR MAN'S GUARDIAN,

A WEEKLY PAPER FOR THE PEOPLE.

This Paper (after sustaining a Government persecution of three years and a half duration, in which upwards of 500 persons were unjustly imprisoned, and cruelly treated for vending it) was, on the Trial of an Ex-Officio Information filed by His Majesty's Attorney-General against Henry Hetherington, IN THE COURT OF EXCHEQUER, *Before* LORD LYNDHURST *and a Special Jury*, DECLARED TO BE A STRICTLY LEGAL PUBLICATION.

Printed and Published by H. Hetherington, 126, Strand.

No. 161.] *Saturday, July 5, 1834.* [Price 1d.

PROGRESS OF DESPOTISM IN AMERICA. THE MIDDLE CLASSES SHOWN TO BE THE REAL AUTHORS OF SLAVERY IN ALL NATIONS. READ AND LEARN, &c.

Friends, Brethren, and Fellow-Countrymen,

In these dreadful times when liberty is, as it were, hunted out of the world, when the best part of mankind is every where trampled on by the worst, it is some consolation to turn our eyes to America. We have received a file of New York papers, from which we glean much that is encouraging, though (we regret to say) not unmixed with much that is the reverse. The usurers and the producers are fairly committed in that country. The bank question is no other than a

oppression engender that almost despair which animates armed citizens to rush on bayonets. It is said the peo[…] France are turbulent, seditious, and uneasy. So are the […] of Ireland, and so are those of every other country whe[…] is the spirit of men abiding, and abuses of authority t[…] into action. The end of all government is the hap[…] mankind, so far as that depends on those enjoyments equally essential to all, namely, the ordinary necessa[…] lodging, and clothing. Whenever the ordinances an[…] of government become so perverted from their orig[…] as to create two orders of society, one consisting […] revel in all the luxuries, and the other of the ma[…] indispensible necessaries of life, there is no oth[…] that this is a bad government. There must b[…] cally wrong in its principles, or vitiated in[…] expounders of that perverted science called p[…] it down as their first principle that labour[…]

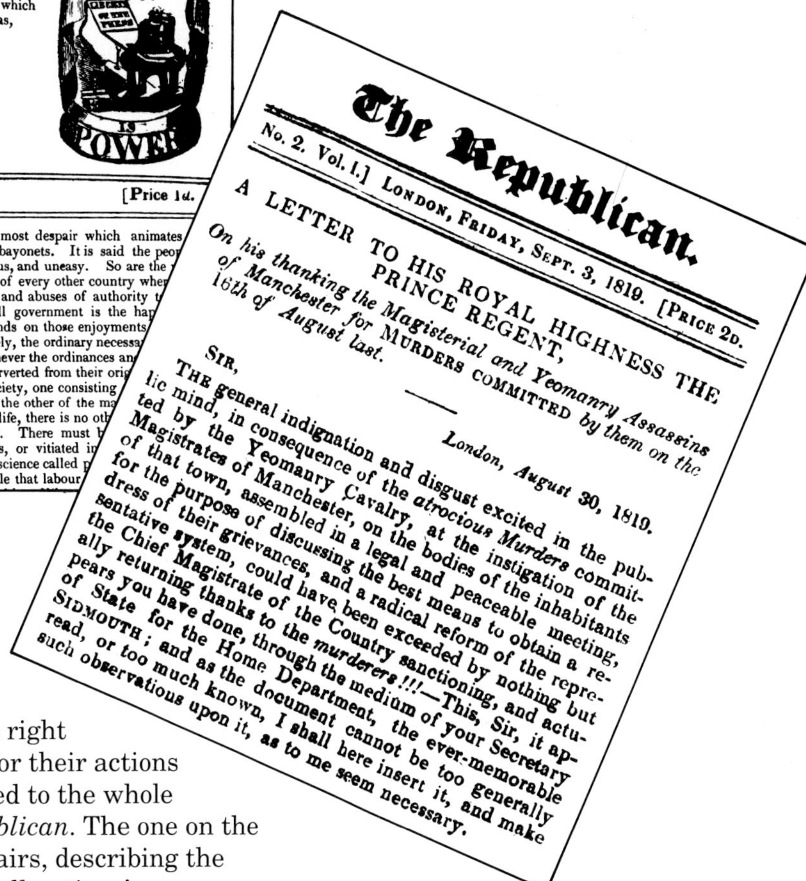

The Republican.

No. 2. Vol. I.] LONDON, FRIDAY, SEPT. 3, 1819. [PRICE 2D.

A LETTER TO HIS ROYAL HIGHNESS THE PRINCE REGENT,

On his thanking the Magisterial and Yeomanry Assassins of Manchester for MURDERS COMMITTED *by them on the 16th of August last.*

London, August 30, 1819.

SIR,

THE general indignation and disgust excited in the public mind, in consequence of the *atrocious Murders* committed by the Yeomanry Cavalry, at the instigation of the Magistrates of Manchester, on the bodies of the inhabitants of that town, assembled in a legal and peaceable meeting, for the purpose of discussing the best means to obtain a redress of their grievances, and a radical reform of the representative system, could have been exceeded by nothing but the Chief Magistrate of the Country sanctioning, and actually returning thanks to the *murderers!!!*—This, Sir, it appears you have done, through the medium of your Secretary of State for the Home Department, the ever-memorable SIDMOUTH; and as the document cannot be too generally read, or too much known, I shall here insert it, and make such observations upon it, as to me seem necessary.

Your answer should have been something like 'a challenge to the existing political system' or 'the growth of working-class agitation'. Both newspapers make radical criticisms of the way the country is run – in other words they are fundamentally opposed to the existing system of government. The title of the one on the right shows that, as well as attacking the authorities for their actions at the Peterloo massacre of 1819, it is also opposed to the whole monarchical system of government, i.e. it is *republican*. The one on the left is also very hostile to the existing state of affairs, describing the 'middle classes' as 'the real authors of slavery in all nations'.

Criticisms of this kind were not unknown before the late 18th century, but they had been very rare. What was new about the period from the late 18th century onwards was that such criticisms were made more frequently. What was also new was the way opponents of the existing system began to organise themselves to try to bring about change.

Both newspapers shown on this page saw themselves as the champions of the working class. It was this group, during these years, that came to concern itself more and more with politics. Working-class people came to feel that they had rights that were being ignored. They began to attack a society that seemed to be organised in the interests of a wealthy minority. They became more confident that *they* themselves had the power to do something about this.

Working-class people agitated for change in many different ways. Some concentrated on trying to bring about political reforms. These included the Chartists, whom you will be studying in the second of the two assignments (12.2) in this chapter. Chartism was probably the largest and most organised working-class movement that Britain had ever seen. Others put all their efforts into trade unionism, organising groups of workers to press for better wages and conditions. The first assignment (12.1) looks at some of the earliest trade unions, operating at a time when their very existence was against the law. Both assignments encourage you to ask why all this working-class protest began to take place during this particular period. To what extent, for example, was it a result of the industrial revolution?

Assignment 12.1

'A very general spirit of combination': early trade unions and the law

At the end of the 18th century the word 'combination' was used to describe associations of workers designed to try to obtain higher wages and better conditions. Such 'combinations' had existed in a small way for some time. Many grew out of the friendly societies that had developed during the 18th century among groups of skilled workers. As you will see from the sources, 'combinations' were particularly active during the 1790s. The authorities were very worried about all this activity and in 1799–1800 passed the Combination acts banning all combinations aimed at securing better wages or conditions. These laws greatly restricted the activities of trade unions. But they did not put a stop to them.

The purpose of the assignment is to make you think about the reasons why these combinations developed at this time. It is also concerned with examining the attitudes of the authorities towards them.

Source A

From a letter sent by two Lancashire Justices of the Peace to Henry Dundas, Home Secretary, 19 July 1791

...The trade of this County is wonderfully prosperous. It produces its ***attendant evils****; amongst those I include a very numerous and* ***foreign*** *population (especially from Ireland) ... These men are full of money from the high rate of wages, and are frequently filled with liquor, and engaged in very desperate* ***affrays.*** *We have also now a very general spirit of combination amongst all sorts of labourers and artisans, who are in a state of disaffection to all legal control. The introduction of machinery to* ***abridge labour*** *in weaving, is also a subject, at this time, of peculiar disgust and jealousy. And I fear, the* ***example of Birmingham****, and an unhappy party spirit about the Revolution in France, heightened by* ***the meetings on the 14th*** *(of this month) ... has added to the general ill-humour and may be a pretext for mischief ...*

attendant evils: evils resulting from the fact that the county was prosperous
affrays: fights
abridge labour: reduce the number of labourers that are needed
the example of Birmingham: recent riots in that town
the meetings on the 14th (July): meetings to celebrate the storming of the Bastille in Paris on 14th July, 1789 (one of the first major events of the French Revolution)

Source B

From a letter sent by William Blackburn in South Shields to Rowland Burdon, MP for County Durham, 16 December 1801

In consequence of a reduction of wages being signified to the ***shipwrights*** *of this place, they chose to strike, as it is termed, and thereafter did assemble in large bodies, preventing any of their own (people) working, and even attempting to decoy the foreman, but in consequence of Messrs. Bulmer acting spiritedly, as appears by the enclosed handbill No.1, the tumult in the place subsided, but they still continue off work, and have sent a threatening letter to Mr. Joseph Bulmer, a copy enclosed, No.2 – and Messrs. Bulmer have since issued the advertisement No.3. In addition to which, they and the other gentlemen of this place, especially the shipbuilders and dockowners have to request you will immediately apply to the* ***Secretary of State*** *to* ***second*** *such advertisement with his Majesty's pardon and reward, for such proceedings, unless speedily checked, may end in serious consequences.*

Three items were enclosed with this letter, as mentioned above:

No.1

A printed notice

Town Hall, South Shields

We, the undernamed persons, shipwrights, resident in South Shields, do acknowledge that we have committed a great abuse in (secretly) entering the dockyard of Messrs. Bulmer in South Shields, and endeavouring to prevail on the foremen to quit their work; and declare, in this public manner, our thanks to Messrs. Bulmer for their withdrawing the prosecution commenced against us, on the late Act of Parliament for preventing unlawful combinations of workmen: and promise that we will not invade the peace of the town or neighbourhood by a repetition of these acts.

We also consent that this declaration shall be published by a circulation of ***handbills****.*

Peter Lawson, Thomas Hunter, James Hunter, Thomas Whiteman, William Newton, John Rutter

Witnesses, Charles Cockerill, Jonathan Cockerill, 9 December, 1801

No.2

Copy of a note

You Bulmer, if you do not give the carpenters a guinea a week as sure as Hell is hot O before winter is done you must be shot O ...

No.3

A printed notice offering:

a"reward of 100 guineas for information leading to the conviction of the writer of the threatening letter, which was put under the door of the Compting-house of Messrs. R. Bulmer & Co., and found on the 14th."

shipwrights: shipbuilders (workers)
Secretary of State: Home Secretary
second: support
handbills: notices

Source C

From a letter sent by Henry Dundas, Home Secretary, to Henry Blundell, Mayor of Liverpool, 30 May 1792

I have been favoured with your letter of the 27th, giving an account of the combinations which have taken place among the carpenters and masters of the coal ***flats*** *at Liverpool for the purpose of obtaining an advance of wages, and of your proceedings in consequence.*

Although there may not be any immediate disposition to riot among these people, it appears .. to be extremely necessary that you should be watchful over their conduct, and that you should pursue every legal and constitutional means of suppressing such combinations and of bringing the ring leaders to punishment. From the disposition which has recently been shown by a certain class of people at Manchester, it is not conceived to be advisable at this moment to remove any part of the troops now stationed there from thence unless in a case of absolute necessity, and if such necessity should hereafter exist ... the Commanding Officer at that place will have instructions to comply with any requisition from you for a detachment from the forces under his orders.

flats: flat bottomed boats

Source E (below and right)

From the Articles (or rules) of the Society of Journeymen Brush-makers, 1806. Journeymen were skilled workers who had completed their apprenticeship. At this time the letter 's' was sometimes printed as 'f'.

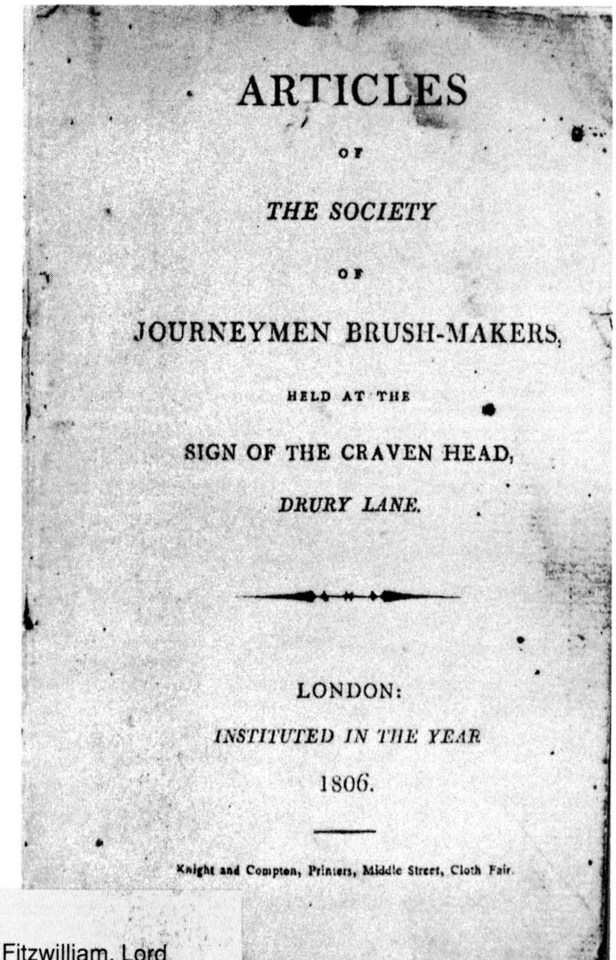
ARTICLES

OF

THE SOCIETY

OF

JOURNEYMEN BRUSH-MAKERS,

HELD AT THE

SIGN OF THE CRAVEN HEAD,

DRURY LANE.

LONDON:

INSTITUTED IN THE YEAR

1806.

Knight and Compton, Printers, Middle Street, Cloth Fair.

Source D

From a letter sent by William Cookson, Mayor of Leeds, to Earl Fitzwilliam, Lord Lieutenant of the West Riding of Yorkshire, 8 September, 1802

the evils call aloud for a cure ... privileges, time, mode of labour, rate, who shall be employed, etc., etc., – all are now dependent upon the ***fiats*** *of our workmen, beyond all appeal; and all branches are struggling for their share of these new powers. It is now a confirmed thing that a bricklayer, mason, carpenter, wheelwright, etc., shall have 3s. per week higher wages in Leeds or in Manchester than at Wakefield, York, Hull, Rochdale, or any adjacent town. It is in order too that bricklayers' and masons' labourers at Leeds shall have 2s. per week extra. No workman will or dare deviate from these terms, no matter whence he comes, and there arrived here last week two delegates from Carlisle on their way to Manchester, summoned by the Lancashire cotton printers, to agree upon certain advances in their wages, who made no secret of their mission ...*

fiats: orders

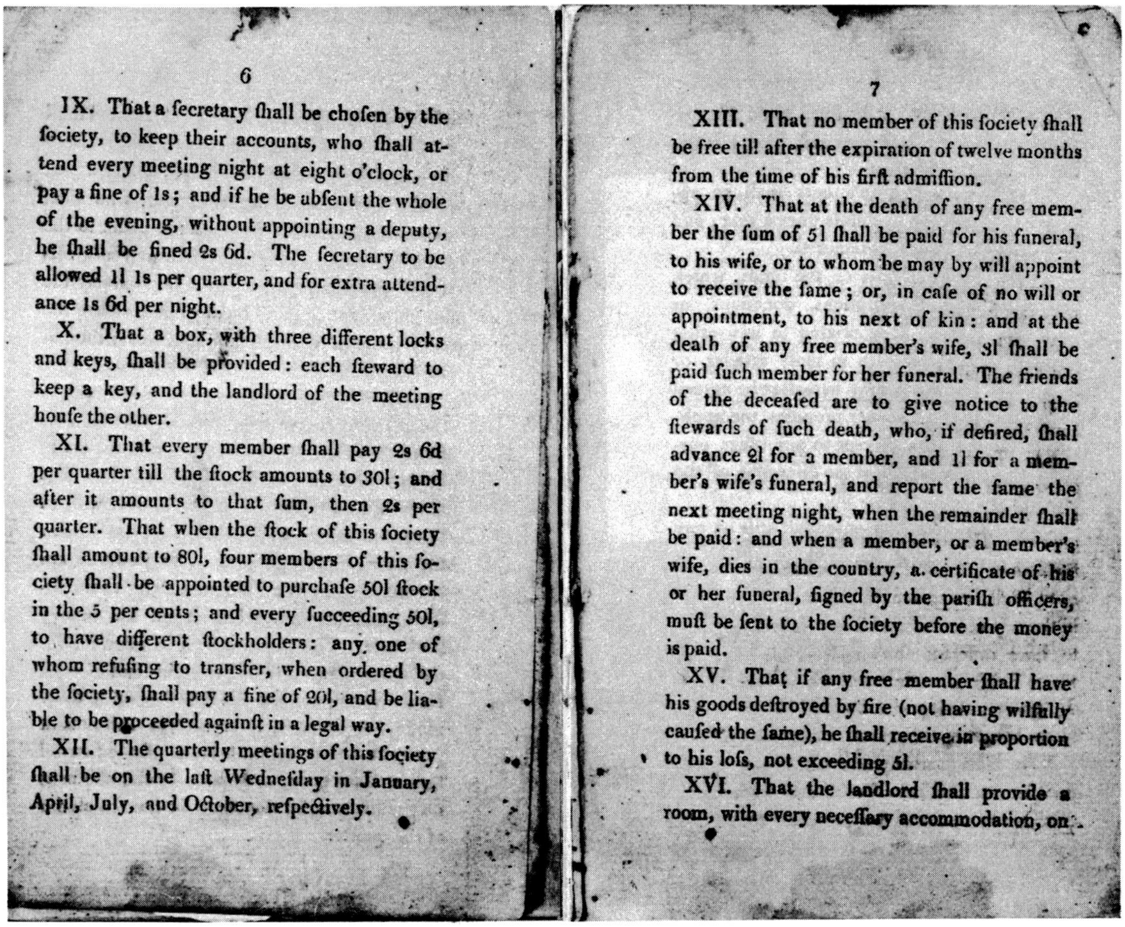

6

IX. That a ſecretary ſhall be choſen by the ſociety, to keep their accounts, who ſhall attend every meeting night at eight o'clock, or pay a fine of 1s; and if he be abſent the whole of the evening, without appointing a deputy, he ſhall be fined 2s 6d. The ſecretary to be allowed 1l 1s per quarter, and for extra attendance 1s 6d per night.

X. That a box, with three different locks and keys, ſhall be provided: each ſteward to keep a key, and the landlord of the meeting houſe the other.

XI. That every member ſhall pay 2s 6d per quarter till the ſtock amounts to 30l; and after it amounts to that ſum, then 2s per quarter. That when the ſtock of this ſociety ſhall amount to 80l, four members of this ſociety ſhall be appointed to purchaſe 50l ſtock in the 5 per cents; and every ſucceeding 50l, to have different ſtockholders: any one of whom refuſing to transfer, when ordered by the ſociety, ſhall pay a fine of 20l, and be liable to be proceeded againſt in a legal way.

XII. The quarterly meetings of this ſociety ſhall be on the laſt Wedneſday in January, April, July, and October, reſpectively.

7

XIII. That no member of this ſociety ſhall be free till after the expiration of twelve months from the time of his firſt admiſſion.

XIV. That at the death of any free member the ſum of 5l ſhall be paid for his funeral, to his wife, or to whom he may by will appoint to receive the ſame; or, in caſe of no will or appointment, to his next of kin: and at the death of any free member's wife, 3l ſhall be paid ſuch member for her funeral. The friends of the deceaſed are to give notice to the ſtewards of ſuch death, who, if deſired, ſhall advance 2l for a member, and 1l for a member's wife's funeral, and report the ſame the next meeting night, when the remainder ſhall be paid: and when a member, or a member's wife, dies in the country, a certificate of his or her funeral, ſigned by the pariſh officers, muſt be ſent to the ſociety before the money is paid.

XV. That if any free member ſhall have his goods deſtroyed by fire (not having wilfully cauſed the ſame), he ſhall receive in proportion to his loſs, not exceeding 5l.

XVI. That the landlord ſhall provide a room, with every neceſſary accommodation, on

Activities

1 Study Source A. Why do you think there was a 'spirit of combination' among labourers at this particular time? Refer both to Source A and to your background knowledge.

2 Study Sources A, B, C and E.

(i) What do you learn from these sources about the purposes for which 'combinations' were formed? Refer in detail to each source in turn.

(ii) What similarities and differences do you notice between these purposes?

3 Study Source C. Give an account *in your own words* of the events referred to in this source.

4 'The Combination Acts of 1799–1800 may have made life more difficult for some trade unionists, but their importance has sometimes been exaggerated.' Do Sources B, C, D and E support this statement?

5 What do you learn from these sources about (a) the attitudes of the authorities towards combinations and (b) the actions taken to deal with them?

6 Are there any problems in using sources such as these when studying the early history of trade unionism? Refer to the sources in support of your answer.

Assignment 12.2
The Chartists are coming, get out of the way ...

This assignment is about the aims of Chartism. That might sound fairly straightforward. Anyone who has studied Chartism is soon familiar with the Six Points of the Charter (shown in Source A). It is not enough, however, just to be able to recite the Six Points. It is also necessary to find out *why* they were important to Chartists and what they meant to different members of the movement.

Once you begin to study Chartism you will discover that there were many different kinds of Chartists. Some were socialists; others were very hostile to socialism. Some supported revolution; others strongly opposed any suggestion of violence. Some were preoccupied with getting rid of the new Poor Law; others were more interested in trade unionism – or in one of many other causes such as factory reform, the repeal of the Corn Laws, and freedom of the press. In practice Chartism varied enormously from place to place, from social group to social group, and from individual to individual. All Chartists, however, agreed that the existing state of affairs was drastically in need of reform. All rallied in support of the Charter.

The following sources date from different periods in the history of Chartism. Source A (or slightly different versions of it) was on display throughout the period. Sources B and C were written in the late 1830s when the movement had just got underway. Source D refers to the last great Chartist petition of 1848 and was obviously composed at the time. All sources tell you something about the hopes, aims or feelings of the Chartists.

The Six Points
OF THE
PEOPLE'S
CHARTER.

1. A VOTE for every man twenty-one years of age, of sound mind, and not undergoing punishment for crime.

2. THE BALLOT.—To protect the elector in the exercise of his vote.

3. NO PROPERTY QUALIFICATION for Members of Parliament —thus enabling the constituencies to return the man of their choice, be he rich or poor.

4. PAYMENT OF MEMBERS, thus enabling an honest tradesman, working man, or other person, to serve a constituency, when taken from his business to attend to the interests of the country.

5. EQUAL CONSTITUENCIES, securing the same amount of representation for the same number of electors, instead of allowing small constituencies to swamp the votes of large ones.

6. ANNUAL PARLIAMENTS, thus presenting the most effectual check to bribery and intimidation, since though a constituency might be bought once in seven years (even with the ballot), no purse could buy a constituency (under a system of universal suffrage) in each ensuing twelvemonth; and since members, when elected for a year only, would not be able to defy and betray their constituents as now.

Source A
A handbill (or public notice) giving the Six Points of the People's Charter

Source B

From a pamphlet issued by the Kettering Radical Association in 1839. The pamphlet consists of an open letter to a local gentleman laying down the claims of the Chartists.

First; We claim to have a voice in the making of the laws under which we live ...

Secondly; We claim that all votes for Members of Parliament shall be taken by Ballot ...

Thirdly; We claim the abolition of all property qualifications for the ***legislative office*** *...*

Fourthly; We claim that every member of parliament shall receive a salary out of the public treasury ...

Fifthly; We claim that parliaments shall be elected annually ...

Sixthly; We claim that the country shall be divided into equal electoral districts...

Seventhly; We claim to be allowed to purchase food for ourselves and families wherever we can procure it cheapest ...

Eighthly; We claim that the working-classes shall be exempted from all beyond the just proportion of the burdens of the State ...

Ninthly; We claim that the Church shall be wholly separated from the State ...

Tenthly; We claim the total repeal of the New Poor Law, and the enactment of a ***statute*** *which while it shall secure the rights of property, shall also recognise and protect the rights of those who have it not ...*

Finally, we appeal to your sense of justice. Place yourself, so far as imagination will enable you, in the condition of (the poor) ... Imagine yourself doomed to endure the heat of the summer's sun, and the severity of the winter's cold, and then, as the reward of your toil, compelled to subsist on less than a ***sufficiency*** *of the coarsest bread; or imagine yourself confined to your workshop from earliest morn to an hour not far from midnight, leaving scarcely enough time for necessary repose ... imagine that your aged parents, or your widowed mother, after having contributed sixty years of toil ... were starving on the pittance allowed them by a board of Guardians ... and as you trace the dark outlines of this appalling picture, remember that though to you it is an imaginary case, this, and worse than this, is a sad reality to tens of thousands of your brethren ...*

legislative office: member of parliament
statute: law
sufficiency: enough

Source C

From a report in a Chartist newspaper of a speech given by the Chartist leader J. R. Stephens on Kersal Moor, near Manchester, 24 September 1838

This question of Universal Suffrage was a knife and fork question after all; this question was a bread and cheese question, notwithstanding all that had been said against it; and if any man ask him what he meant by Universal Suffrage, he would answer, that every working man in the land had a right to have a good coat to his back, a good dinner upon his table, and no more work than was necessary for keeping him in health, and as much wages for that work as would keep him in plenty, and afford him the enjoyment of all the blessings of life which a reasonable man could desire. (Tremendous cheers.)

Source D

From a contemporary report of a public meeting of Chartists at Stockport, late 1830s

MR. CAMPBELL then rose, and observed that the misery and distress of this country were to be subjected to four causes. First, **want** of education; second, want of employment; third, low wages; and fourth, competition of machinery against manual labour ... He contended that there was no hope for the people, so long as society was carried on under the competitive system ...

MR. LEACH, who gave a clear definition of the Charter, proving it to be founded on natural law.. He thought Mr. Campbell's argument, relative to education did not stand good ... many of the greatest tyrants in existence were the best scholars. He contended that the want of political power was the greatest evil to the mass of the people ... He would say let the people get political power ... The Charter was only a means to an end.

want: lack

Source E

A Chartist song of 1848

The Chartists are Coming

What a row and a rumpus there is I declare,
Tens of thousands are flocking everywhere;
To petition the Parliament, onward they steer,
The Chartists are coming, oh dear, oh dear,
To demand equal justice, their freedom and rights,
Pump-handles and broomsticks, lawk, how they can fight;
The nation, they say, is o'erwhelmèd with grief,
A peck loaf for two pence and four pounds of beef.

Chorus
Hurrah for old England and liberty sweet,
The land that we live in and plenty to eat;
We shall ever remember this wonderful day,
The Chartists are coming, get out of the way.

Such a number together was never yet seen,
Hurrah for the Charter and God save the Queen;
And when that the Charter old England has got,
We'll have stunning good beer at three halfpence a pot.
A loaf for a penny, a pig for a crown,
And gunpowder tea at five farthings a pound;
Instead of red herrings we'll live on fat geese,
And get lots of young women at two pence apiece.

The bakers and grocers, look how they do laugh,
With dustmen and coalheavers, armed with a staff;
Five thousand old women, oh, how they do sing,
With frying pans, **fenders**, and big rolling pins.
There's **Russell** and **Bobby**, **old Nosey** and **Hume**,
With pistols and bayonets, big muskets and brooms;
Load away, fire away, and chatter and jaw,
Shoot at a donkey and knock down a crow.

See the lads of old **Erin** for liberty crow,
Smith O'Brien for ever and Erin-go-bragh;
Peace and contentment, then none can we blame,
Plenty of labour and paid for the same.
Some are rolling in riches and luxury too.

While millions are starving, with nothing to do;
Through the nation prosperity soon will be seen,
Hurrah for Great Britain and God save the Queen.

To **Kennington Common** in droves they repair,
'Cause Smith O'Brien and **Feargus** are there;
A-telling the story would reach, sir, indeed,
From the Land's End of England to Berwick on Tweed.
The Charter, the Charter, or England shall quake,
I wish they may get it, and no grand mistake,
Then Feargus shall be a prime minister keen,
And Smith O'Brien a page to the Queen.

Such **constables** there is in London, now mark,
There's tailors and shoemakers, labourers and clerks,
Gaslightmen, pickpockets, and firemen, too,
Greengrocers and hatters, pork butchers and Jews,
Lollypop merchants and masons a lot,
And the covey that hollers 'Baked taters all hot.'
They're sworn to protect us and keep well the peace,
To frighten the Chartists and help the police.

fenders: metal surrounds for fires
Russell: Lord John Russell, Prime Minister in 1848
Bobby: Sir Robert Peel, Conservative Prime Minister from 1841 to 1846
old Nosey: the Duke of Wellington
Hume: Joseph Hume, radical middle-class politician
Erin: Ireland (Erin-go-bragh: Ireland for ever)
Smith O'Brien: Irish nationalist and Chartist
Kennington Common: site of the big Chartist demonstration in 1848
Feargus: Feargus O'Connor, Chartist leader
constables: the song refers here to the special constables who were sworn in to help control the Kennington demonstration

Activities

1 Study Source A. Explain in your own words how each of the Six Points of the Charter was intended to give the working classes more political power.

2 Study Sources B and C. In what ways and to what extent do these sources share the same hopes and aims? Refer in detail to the sources in support of your answer.

3 (i) Which of the two speakers in Source D was a socialist? Give reasons for your answer.

(ii) Do any of the other sources contain socialist ideas? Explain your answer.

4 Study Source E.

(i) Write short notes on all the main historical references in this song, e.g. 'line 3: petition – a petition presented to parliament asking it to accept the Six Points of the Charter'.

(ii) How useful is this source to someone studying the attitudes of the Chartists? Explain your answer, referring in detail to the source.

5 Referring to your background knowledge, give any other reasons that help to explain support for Chartism in the late 1830s and 1840s.

Further activities

1 Choose *three* events or developments in the history of trade unionism during the first half of the 19th century (e.g. the repeal of the Combination acts, the transportation of the Tolpuddle Martyrs, etc.). In each case describe the event or development, explain why it occurred and comment on its effects.

2 Find *three* popular songs of the 18th or early 19th centuries that refer to changes taking place at the time.

(i) In the case of each song (a) explain the background to the song and (b) say how useful you think it is as an historical source.

(ii) Is one of the songs more useful than the others? Explain your answer.

3 (i) If you were studying the development of Chartism in a particular local area, what questions would you want to ask? (e.g. Which social groups supported Chartism? Was their strong support?).

(ii) If there were Chartists in your own area, try to find out the answers to as many of these questions as you can.

13 *Trade Unionism*
and Working-Class Movements from 1850 to the Present Day

When people think about historical *evidence* they tend to think first about documents and then perhaps about visual sources such as photographs, drawings and cartoons. They often forget about objects (or artefacts), unless of course they are studying early periods where very little written evidence survives. One of the purposes of this chapter is to show you how objects can be a useful source for recent history as well. The objects that you will be studying in Assignment 13.1 are trade union banners. These were made to decorate the meeting rooms of trade union branches and to be carried at demonstrations or on other public occasions. Trade union banners are still in use today – many of them dating from much earlier in the 20th century or even in some cases from the 19th century. Many of them refer to events in the history of the trade union movement. Looking at these banners reminds many trade union members that they are part of a long tradition – a tradition of both co-operation and struggle.

During the second half of the 19th century and the first half of the 20th century there was a very big increase in the proportion of workers belonging to trade unions. The legal position of trade unions was also much stronger at the end of that period than at the beginning. This strengthening of the trade union movement was closely associated, at least from the late 19th century onwards, with the rise of the Labour Party. This was the first major political party to identify itself with the interests of the 'working classes'. Labour was briefly in office in 1924 and again in 1929–31, but did not win an overall majority in the House of Commons until 1945 when it embarked on a major programme of reform designed to improve the lot of the working classes.

People in modern Britain disagree, sometimes violently, about the extent to which trade union and working-class movements have brought benefits to the country. Some see trade unions as a disruptive force that, by unsettling the economy, has harmed the interests of the working class. Others argue that without trade unions wages and conditions would be far worse than they are today. People also disagree about the extent to which trade unionism and working-class movements have brought about radical change. From one point of view the political influence of the working-classes is far greater now than ever before. From another point of view the changes that have taken place have done little to alter the distribution of wealth within Britain or to allow the working classes to influence the way the economy develops. The second of the two assignments in this chapter (13.2) examines an occasion when the trade union movement both demonstrated its importance and at the same time was forced to recognise the limitations on its power.

Assignment 13.1
Trade union banners

A recent book on trade union banners estimated that approximately 10 000 banners were produced between 1832 and 1939. About three quarters of these seem to have been made by one firm of banner-makers – George Tutill of City Road, London. Of the few that survive, most belong to branches of mining unions. Many of the surviving banners date from the 1890s or from the period 1910–26. Most were made in a very similar style, which did not change much over the years.

This assignment encourages you to look very closely at some of these banners and to see what you can learn from them about the attitudes of those for whom they were made. It draws attention to some of the problems of using this kind of evidence. It is also intended to encourage you to go out and look at some of these banners for yourselves – or at least to notice them and to think about them when they appear on your television screen.

Source A
A banner made in 1896 for the Barrow branch of the Yorkshire Miners' Association

Source B
The Cleveland district banner of the Associated Iron and Steel Workers of Great Britain, 1897. The portraits at the top of the banner represent the general secretary of the union (top left) and the iron worker who founded the original union in 1862 (top right). The scene below shows a meeting between representatives of employers and workers.

Source C

The banner of the Lofthouse branch of the Yorkshire Miners Association

Source D

A banner of the Follonsby Lodge of the Durham Miners' Association, c.1924. The figures on the banner represent: Lenin, the Bolshevik leader; James Connolly, one of the leaders of the Irish nationalist Easter Rising of 1916; A. J. Cook, the miners' leader; Keir Hardie, socialist pioneer; and George Harvey, a local miner. By 1947 the figures of Lenin, Connolly and Harvey had been painted over.

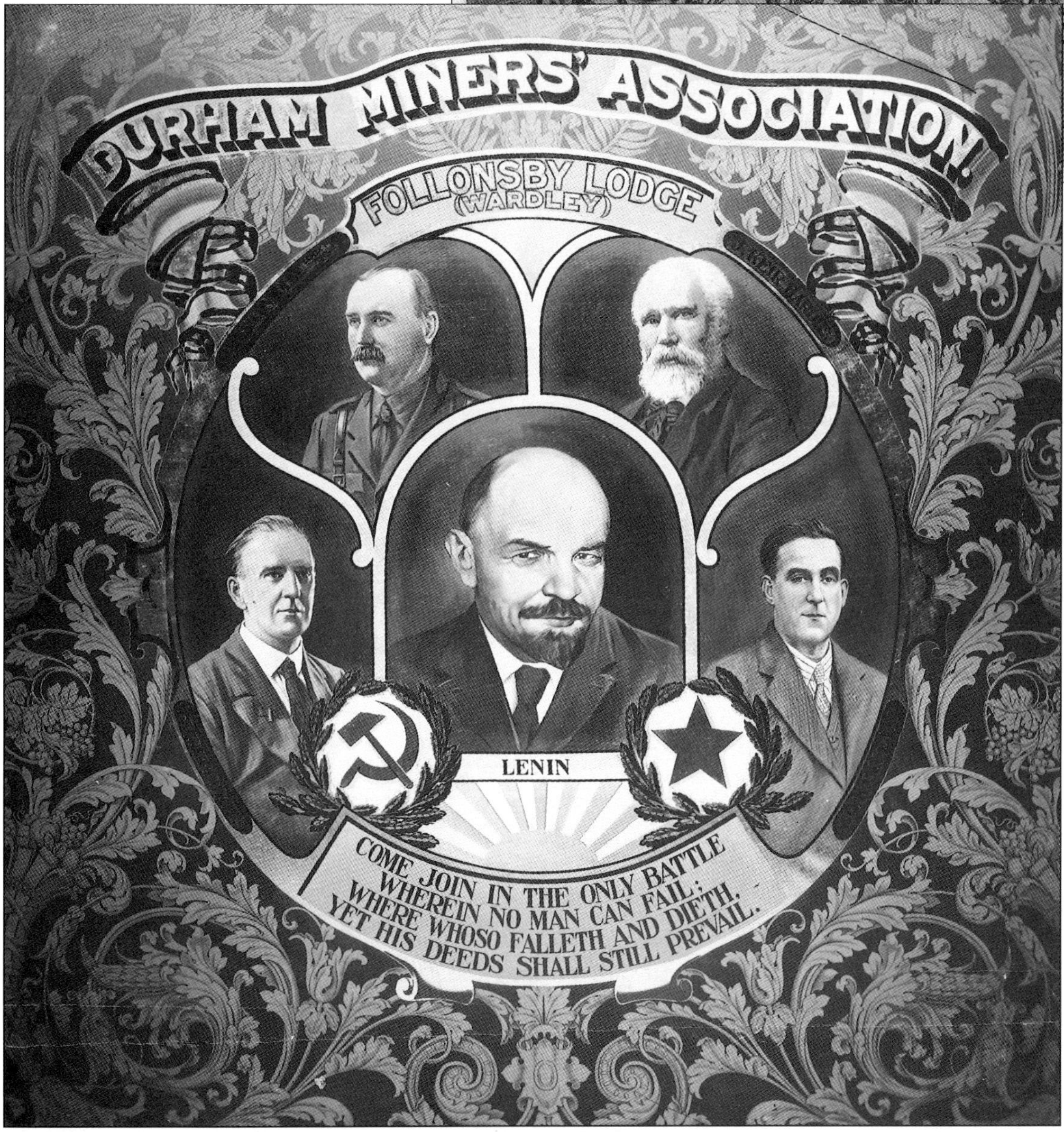

Source E
The banner of the Wombwell, Yorkshire, branch of the National Union of Mineworkers

Activities

1 What do you learn from these sources about the purposes for which trade unions existed? Refer in detail to the sources in support of your answer.

2 What is meant by 'militant' trade unionism? Do any of these banners suggest that their unions were 'militant' in their attitudes? Refer to the sources in support of your answer.

3 Do these sources suggest anything about the *political* views held by trade unionists? Support your answer by reference to the sources.

4 What methods are used by the banner-makers to put across their message? Refer to the sources in detail.

5 (i) Does the fact that most trade union banners were made by one firm make any difference to the value of these banners as sources? Explain your answer.

(ii) What are the advantages and disadvantages of trade union banners as pieces of historical evidence? Refer to the sources in support of your answer.

Assignment 13.2
The General Strike of 1926

People in Britain reacted in very different ways to the General Strike of 1926. This assignment looks at the different reactions. It encourages you to examine sources closely in order to identify the bias and viewpoint of particular writers.

The General Strike was the climax of several years of industrial unrest. At the centre of this unrest were the coal miners' unions. The immediate cause of the General Strike was the publication of the Samuel Report of 1926 which, among other changes (some of which were more favourable to miners), recommended a cut in miners' wages. The mine owners were quick to take up this suggestion, demanding at the same time an increase in working hours, i.e. more money for less work. The miners' leader, A. J. Cook, pledged 'Not a penny off the pay, not a minute on the day'.

Via the Trades Union Congress (TUC), Cook and the miners asked for the support of other unions. This support was given and on 4 May the General Strike began. Despite massive support, it only lasted nine days. At the end of this time the TUC agreed to a compromise and urged member unions to return to work. The miners resented this 'betrayal', remaining on strike for another three months.

The General Strike demonstrated the ability of the trade union movement to mobilise large numbers of people in support of its cause. It also showed how reluctant some trade unionists were to use this ability to full effect. Above all perhaps it showed how difficult it was to intimidate a government that had all the forces of law and order at its disposal. The collapse of the strike was followed in 1927 by the Trade Disputes Act which made general strikes illegal.

Source A
From a letter sent by Stanley Baldwin, the Prime Minister, to the TUC, 2 May 1926

It has come to the knowledge of the Government, not only that specific instructions have been sent under the authority of the Executives of Trade Unions represented at the Conference, convened by the General Council of the Trades Union Congress, directing their members in several of the most vital industries and services of the country to carry out a general strike on Tuesday next, but that ***overt*** *acts have already taken place ... Such action involves a challenge to the constitutional rights and freedom of the nation.*

overt: open

Source B

From the manifesto of the Miners' Federation, 5 May 1926

Comrades. – The struggle has begun. Menaced with an onslaught on their standards of life by the mine-owners and the Government, the Miners' Federation of Great Britain submitted their case to the judgment of their fellow trade unionists. The General Council and Conference of Trade Union Executives considered it with a full sense of their grave responsibility and pronounced it just beyond all possibility of question ...

We have laboured for a peaceful settlement, but the Government, not only by its words but by its actions, has shown only too plainly that peace is not what it desires. In insisting that the miners should pledge themselves to accept a reduction in wages before even entering negotiations, it advanced an unheard-of demand which no body of Trade Unionists could accept. In suddenly breaking off negotiations with the General Council and the Miners' Federation on Sunday night, it revealed its determination to force upon the Trade Union Movement a struggle for which the Government had long prepared.

Source C

From a sermon delivered at High Mass in Westminster Cathedral on Sunday 9 May 1926 by Cardinal Bourne

It is necessary that Catholics should have before their minds the moral principles which are involved:

1. There is no moral justification for a general strike of this character. It is a direct challenge to lawfully constituted authority, and inflicts, without adequate reason, immense discomfort and injury on millions of our fellow-countrymen. It is therefore a sin against the obedience which we owe to God, who is the source of that authority, and against the charity and brotherly love which are due to our **brethren**.

2. All are bound to uphold and assist the Government, which is the lawfully constituted authority of the country, and represents, therefore, in its own appointed sphere the authority of God Himself ...

brethren: brothers/fellow human beings

Source D

Published in the *Bulletin* of the St Pancras, London, local strike committee, May 1926

A is for ALL, ALL OUT and ALL WIN,
And down with the blacklegs and scabs who stay in.
B is for Baldwin, the Bosses' Strong Man,
But he's welcome to dig all the coal that he can.
C is for Courage the workers have shown,
Class Conscious and Confident that they'll hold their own.
D is for DOPE that the Government spread –
Dishwash for Duncos and Dubbs – "nuf sed."
E is for Energy that will carry us through,
Everyone class-conscious, steadfast and true.
F is for fight, our fight to the end,
For we're solid together, not an inch will we bend.
G is for Grab-all, the bosses, you know,
Greedy and grasping, one day they must go.
H is Hardship, we all must endure;
However, keep smiling, for Victory is sure.
I is for Interest, Profits and Rent
Into the pockets of the Indolent.
J is for Jix, the stirrer of strife,
Just waiting the chance to have your life.
K is for knife that is wielded by Jix,
Keep yourselves orderly and frustrate his tricks.
L is for London, where the T.U.C. meet,
Leading the workers the bosses to beat.
M is for Miners, for whose rights we must fight,
Maintaining the cause which we know to be right.
N is for Natsopa, who stopped dope from the Boss,
Narking Churchill and Jix, so Baldwin was cross.
O is for O.M.S., the scabbing patrol;
Oh! how they are working, digging the Coal!!
P is for pickets on guard at the gates,
Pulling up blacklegs who scab on their mates.
Q is for Quandary the Government's in,
Quite certain now the workers will win.
R is for Railways that won't run alone,
Ready for workers to run as their own.
S is for Solidarity that is winning our fight;
Stick well together, for Victory's in sight.
T is for Taximen joined in the fray,
Troubling the blacklegs to walk all the way.
U is for Unity, each one for all,
United we stand till the Government fall.
V is for Victory, of which we are sure,
Vanquishing the bosses for evermore.
W is for Workers' Wages and hours,
We are nearing the day when control is ours.
X is for eXit the whole boss class –
Xtra enjoyment for me and my lass.
Y is for Young Workers to whom fighting is new;
Yes, Young, but determined to fight with you.
Z is for Zeal shown by the Vigilance Corps,
Zealous that workers aren't trapped by the law.

Source E

The spoken memories of J. Withers who in 1926 was a member of the London machine branch of the National Society of Operative Printers' Assistants. Quoted in R. A. Leeson, *Strike: A Live History 1887–1971*, 1973

1926 was a real experience. A triumphant disaster if you like. The unions lost, but they frightened the Establishment all right ...

The miners' terrible conditions followed the owners' ultimatum of a wage cut, the government trying to keep the workers down, in fact the whole business of class war being waged when the poorest were weakest, all showed that if ever the unions and the workers in general were to establish some sort of dignity, 1926 was the time. Baldwin, the students and many of the smug white-collar brigade did their damndest to break the strike and I suppose they still live in the belief that they did. But did they? My experience was that Big Business received the biggest shock of its life, that such a situation could happen ...

Activities

1. Which of these sources supported the General Strike and which opposed it? Quote one phrase or sentence from each source that shows whether its author was a supporter or an opponent.
2. Do the opponents of the General Strike oppose it for the same reasons? Refer to the sources in support of your answer.
3. Write short notes on each of the following letters in Source D: D, I, J, N, O, P, X and Z. Refer to textbooks, encyclopaedias and dictionaries to help you explain any reference whose meaning is not clear.
4. Study the sources that you have identified in Question 1 as supporting the General Strike. In what ways do these sources give a similar impression of the General Strike and in what ways do they give a different impression?
5. How valuable are these sources to someone studying the attitudes of the British people towards the General Strike? What other sources might be useful to a student of this topic?

Further activities

1. Study one industrial dispute that has taken place during the period that you have been studying your GCSE History syllabus. Try to find out as much as you can, e.g. from newspapers, about the causes of the dispute, the events of the dispute, and how and why it finally came to an end.

   Compare this industrial dispute with one that took place during the late 19th or early 20th centuries. What differences do you notice between the two disputes and how might you explain these differences?
2. Draw a time chart showing the development of the Labour Party from its formation until the present day. Choose (a) one period when the Labour Party experienced an increase in support and (b) one period when it experienced a decline in support. Give reasons for the increase and decline in support that you have identified.
3. To what extent have working-class people had a say in the running of Britain at each of the following times: 1850; 1880; 1910; 1950; 1980?

   Would you agree that, since 1850, the working classes have become politically much more important?

14 *Social Welfare*

Throughout the period covered by this book the state has always accepted that it is responsible in some way for people who are unable to provide for themselves: the sick, the mentally ill, the old, the orphaned, the unemployed. This has been a constant feature of English life throughout this period (though not always of life in Scotland, where in the 18th and early 19th centuries poor relief was left to the Church). The way in which it has exercised this responsibility – and the extent to which it has done so – has, however, changed dramatically over time. At the end of the 18th century poor relief was mainly the responsibility of *local* government. In the late 20th century many aspects of social welfare are in the hands of *central* government. During the 20th century welfare provision also became much more extensive, culminating eventually in the creation of a welfare state intended to protect its citizens 'from the cradle to the grave'.

The assignments in this chapter examine two crucial turning-points in the development of welfare provision: the Poor Law Amendment Act of 1834 and the Beveridge Report of 1942. As well as being very important in themselves, these two measures also illustrate very different attitudes towards social welfare.

Assignment 14.1
Workhouses after 1834: the poor man's Bastille?

The 'Bastille' was a famous prison in Paris at the time of the French Revolution of 1789. It was a word associated with oppression and cruelty. It was a word sometimes applied in England to the workhouses built after the Poor Law Amendment Act of 1834. Its use shows the very hostile feelings that these workhouses frequently aroused.

There had been workhouses long before 1834. What was new about the Poor Law Amendment Act was the attempt to ensure that poor relief for the able-bodied was *only* given in the workhouse. Before 1834 many able-bodied poor, in times of unemployment, had received what was called 'outdoor relief'. In parts of southern England workers had also, under the Speenhamland system, received supplements to their wages when these had been very low.

The 1834 act was designed to put an end to all this. From now on poor relief would only be available in the workhouse. Conditions in the workhouse would be worse than those among the poorest class of labourers. This, it was hoped, would deter anyone from seeking relief unless they really needed it. The aim was to save money and, in areas where the Speenhamland system had operated, to force employers to pay a living wage. In order to run this new system of poor relief parishes were grouped into *Unions*, each under an elected Board of Guardians. Full-time officials were appointed to administer the new workhouses, under the general supervision of the Poor Law Commission in London.

The Poor Law Amendment Act of 1834 aroused a great deal of controversy. Many contemporary sources are therefore quite strongly biased either in favour of or against the new system. This can make it difficult to find out what conditions were actually like. In addition workhouses varied enormously. They also changed greatly over time, many workouses in the 1870s, for example, being very different from how they had been in the 1830s. One purpose of this assignment is to show you the difficulties of generalising (or making general statements) about workhouse conditions. It is also intended to show you the range of problems with which the workhouses were supposed to deal.

Source A
Poor Law Commissioners, 1830s, quoted in Norman Longmate, *The Workhouse*, 1974

This separation must be entire and absolute between the sexes, who are to live, sleep and take their meals in totally distinct and separate parts of the building, with an enclosed yard for each.

Source B

A drawing of the Fulham and Hammersmith Union workhouse, London, 1849

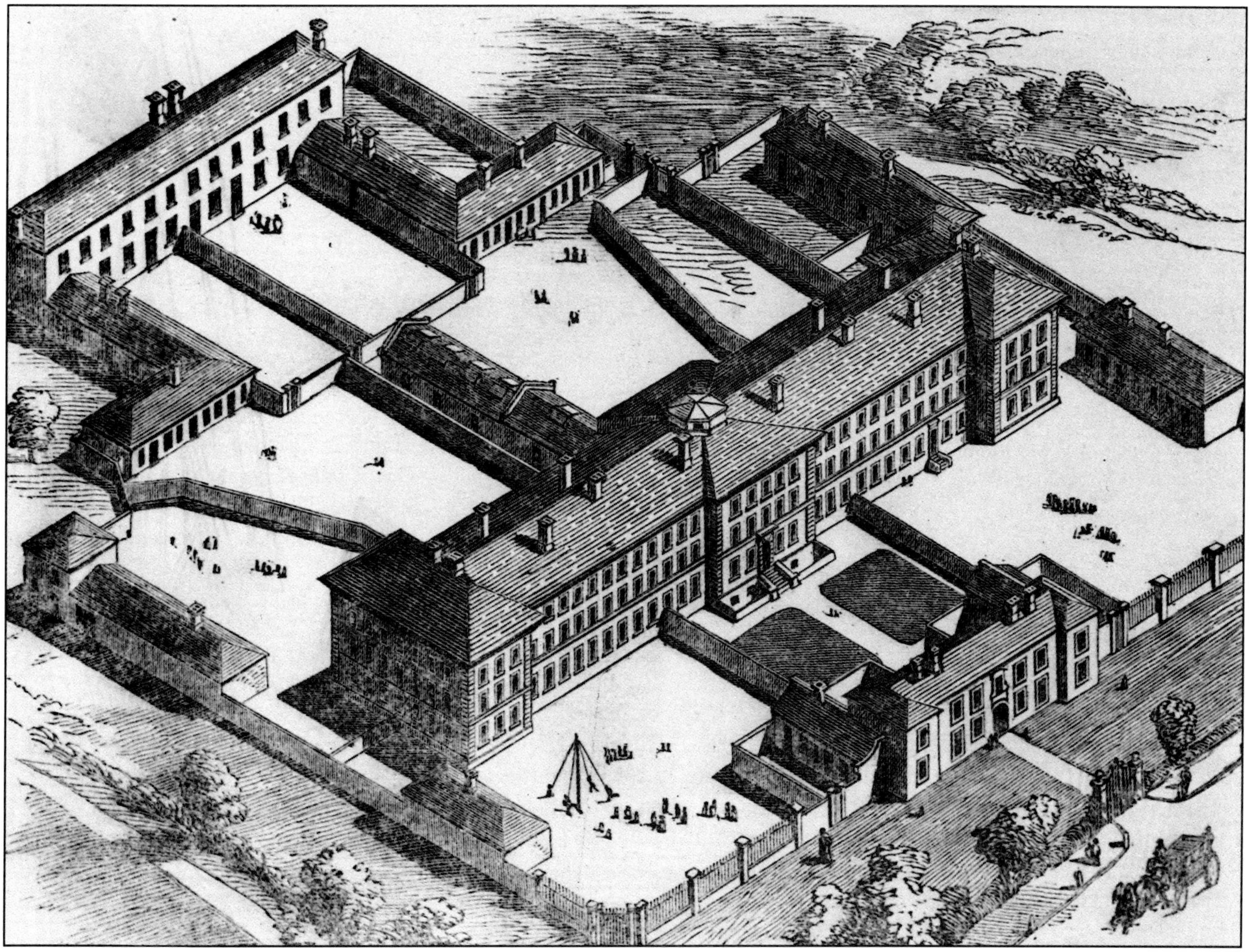

Source C

From a report to the Poor Law Commission by Edward Tufnell, one of its Assistant Commissioners (Inspectors), 1839

A short time back, it was circulated in this county (Kent) that the children in the workhouses were killed to make pies with, while the old when dead were employed to manure the guardians' fields, in order to save the expense of coffins.

Source D

From a report to the Poor Law Commission by an Assistant Commissioner (Inspector), 1840s. The report concerns the workhouse in Bolton, Lancashire.

There is no classification: males and females occupy the same airing grounds and even the same privies. There is no bathroom for cleansing, no probationary ward for receiving the paupers on their admission, which renders it impossible to prevent the spread of any **contagious disorders**. There is no adequate accommodation for the sick poor; and in short the workhouse in its present state cannot be conducted with proper discipline and economy.

contagious disorders: infectious diseases

Source E

From a contemporary account of old people in a workhouse,quoted in Emma Shepherd, *Experiences of a Workhouse Visitor*, 1857

... the listless look – the dull **vacuity** – the lack of all interest, except for the petty details of tea versus gruel – potatoes versus rice! The only object from their windows of moving interest the parish hearse preparing to take away some of their former companions.

vacuity: emptiness

Source F

From the *Report of the Select Committee on Vagrancy* set up by the House of Commons in 1846. This extract is from the evidence of a vagrant known as William Read.

He (Read) applied at Newington about the beginning of this year ... was given half a pound of bread and a rug to cover him. He was then put into a very filthy place; and the moment he got inside the door the bread was snatched away out of his hand and the rug too. He **expostulated** a little concerning it, and they heaved a pail of water over him and two or three began attacking him because he did not belong to the gang.

expostulated: argued

Source G

From a report into the treatment of the mentally ill in workhouses, published in the *Lancet* (a medical journal), 1867. The first part of this extract concerns St Leonard's workhouse, Shoreditch, London.

The general aspect of the wards is one of extreme cheerlessness and desolation ... especially lamentable in the case of the lunatics and imbeciles. Moping about in herds, without any occupation whatever, neither classified nor amused, nor employed – congregated in a miserable day-room where they sit and stare at each other and at the bare walls, and where the monotony is only broken by the occasional excitement due to an epileptic or the gibbering and fitful laughter of some more excitable lunatic. It is quite an oasis in a desert when as at Marylebone, Newington and some other houses we find a garden with swings, bird-cages and rabbit hutches, for the amusement of these poor creatures and a number of pretty pictures pasted upon the walls of their day-room.

Source H

A note delivered by hand to the Poor Law Commission in 1843

Gentlemen, Do for Gods sake take into consideration the sufferings of the poor of Lambeth Work-house ill used and half starved – the Master a perfect brute swearing at sick and aged driving them to Work when scarce able to stand – some of you I know to be men of feeling – my information I know is correct.

Yours respectfully

A Parishioner

P.S. The food scarce fit for Hogs.

Source I

From guidelines issued by the Poor Law Commissioners in 1841

The discipline of a work-house is to be maintained by an undeviating adherence to rules, and a steadiness which defies provocation, while it deliberately enforces obedience to orders by legal and authorised means ... The habits of many of the inmates of a workhouse will often be coarse and depraved, but the conduct of every officer ... should correspond with what those habits ought to be, rather than with what they actually are.

Source J

From M. A. Crowther, *The Workhouse System 1834–1929*, 1981

... in many workhouses after the 1840s conditions were better than in the homes of the very poor.

Activities

1 Study Sources A and B.

(i) Does Source B suggest that the guidelines issued by the Commissioners in Source A were being put into practice?

(ii) What else do you learn from Source B about conditions in this workhouse?

2 What do you learn from Sources A to J about the different types of inmate to be found in 19th century workhouses?

3 Comment on the usefulness of each of Sources C to J for someone studying conditions in 19th century workhouses.

4 Using your answer to Question 3 and referring in detail to all the sources, write an essay in response to the following question:

'Though it is difficult to generalise, conditions in mid-19th century workhouses were often very brutal.' Do you agree?

In tackling this question, make notes on what (if anything) you learn from each source. Then organise these notes into an essay plan.

Assignment 14.2
The Beveridge Report, 1942

Source A
From the *Daily Mirror*, 16 February 1943

Too much has been made of the Beveridge Report. It is no revolutionary document. Mainly it is a co-ordination of existing services with certain modest additions thereto. It is a beginning, not an end, and it must not be confused with reconstruction in the larger sense.

Two weeks after the Beveridge Report was published on 1 December 1942 a national opinion poll found that 95 per cent of those interviewed had heard of the report. This amazingly high percentage illustrates the tremendous interest that it aroused at the time. This interest can be explained partly by Beveridge's recommendations, and in particular by his blueprint for a better post-war world. It can also be explained by the timing of the report. It was published at a crucial point in the war, just when the tide was beginning to turn against Germany and its allies and just when people in Britain were starting to imagine what life after the war would be like. The report gave many people hope that there would be no return to the problems of the 1920s and 1930s. It gave them a new incentive for continuing the long struggle against Nazism.

Most of the Beveridge Report consisted of very detailed and technical proposals for a new scheme of social security. It was not so much these as Beveridge's more general recommendations about 'social progress' that caught the public's attention. These general recommendations were certainly very influential. They led to a whole spate of government white papers during the next few years. These in their turn formed the basis for many of the reforms introduced by the post-war Labour governments of 1945–51.

This assignment has two main purposes: (i) to consider to what extent the Beveridge Report was making 'revolutionary' recommendations (Source A thinks it was; Source B thinks it was not); and (ii) to compare the report's recommendations with what the Labour governments of 1945–51 actually did.

Source B
A David Low cartoon published in 1942

RIGHT TURN

Source C
Extracts from the Beveridge Report, 1942

... social insurance should be treated as one part only of a comprehensive policy of social progress. Social insurance fully developed may provide income security; it is an attack upon Want. But Want is only one of five giants on the road of **reconstruction** and in some ways the easiest to attack. The others are Disease, Ignorance, Squalor and Idleness ...

Under the scheme of social insurance, which forms the main feature of this plan, every citizen of working age will contribute in his appropriate class according to the security that he needs, or as a married woman will have contributions made by the husband. Each will be covered for all his needs by a single weekly contribution on one insurance document. All the principal cash payments – for unemployment, disability and retirement will continue so long as the need lasts, without means test, and will be paid from a Social Insurance Fund built up by contributions from the insured persons, from their employers, if any, and from the State ...

... Any Plan for Social Security in the narrow sense assumes a concerted social policy in many fields ... The plan proposed here involves three particular assumptions so closely related to it that brief discussion is essential for understanding of the plan itself ...

The first of these assumptions underlying the Plan for Social Security is a general scheme of children's allowances. This means that direct provision for the maintenance of dependent children will be made by payment of allowances to those responsible for the care of those children ...

The second of the three assumptions (requires) a national health service for prevention and for cure of disease and disability by medical treatment ... a comprehensive national health service will ensure that for every citizen there is available whatever medical treatment he requires, in whatever form he requires it ... Restoration of a sick person to health is a duty of the State and the sick person, prior to any other consideration ...

Assumpion C (maintenance of employment) requires not the abolition of all unemployment, but the abolition of mass unemployment and of unemployment prolonged year after year for the same individual. In the beginning of compulsory unemployment insurance in 1913 and 1914, it was found that less than 5 per cent of all the unemployment experience in the insured industries occurred after men had been unemployed for as long as 15 weeks. Even if it does not prove possible to get back to that level of employment, it should be possible to make unemployment of any individual for more than 26 weeks continuously a rare thing in normal times ...

Want could have been abolished in Britain just before the war. It can be abolished after the war, unless the British people are and remain very much poorer then than they were before, that is to say unless they remain less productive than they and their fathers were. There is no sense in believing, contrary to experience, that they will and must be less productive. The answer to the question whether freedom from want should be regarded as a post-war aim capable of early attainment **is an affirmative** ...

reconstruction: rebuilding (after the war)
is an affirmative: is 'yes'

Activities

1 Summarise in your own words the main recommendations that are being made in Source C. Use the following headings:

- social insurance
- family allowances
- health
- employment

2 Under each heading compare the Beveridge recommendations with what governments had actually done during the years 1931–39.

3 Use your answers to Questions 1 and 2 to show whether or not you agree with the judgment about the Beveridge Report in Source A.

4 Under each of the headings you have used in Questions 1 and 2 compare the Beveridge recommendations with the actual measures introduced by the Labour governments of 1945–51. Having done this, write a paragraph answering the question: 'To what extent was the Beveridge Report implemented by the post-war Labour government?'

5 Study Sources A and B

(i) Does Source B give a different impression of the Beveridge Report from Source A? Refer in detail to the source in support of your answer.

(ii) Do Sources A and B tell us anything about the public's response to the Beveridge Report?

Further activities

1 Many 19th century workhouse buildings still survive, often as parts of hospitals. Try to find if there are any old workhouses in your local area. Draw and/or photograph the surviving buildings and write a report indicating what you have learnt from them about workhouses. Refer also to any written sources that are available.

2 'Charitable organisations were often more important than government agencies.' Study the relevant sections of your textbooks to see whether you agree with this comment on 19th century social welfare.

3 During the 1980s there was a great deal of discussion about government provision of welfare services. Some Conservative politicians argued strongly in favour of reducing the government's role in welfare provision. Discuss in small groups the arguments for and against such a reduction in government provision. Use your conclusions to prepare for a class debate and then write up individually your report of the arguments for and against.

15 *Education*

Look at the photograph below. It was taken in the late 19th century and shows a class of children at one of the Board schools established after the Education Act of 1870. There are thousands of photographs like this one all over the country. Perhaps someone in your family has something similar.

Photographs like these are useful historical evidence. By studying them we can learn a great deal about conditions in schools 100 years ago. Notice the size of the class – how does it compare with the size of the class you are in today? How did class sizes of this kind affect children's experiences of school? Notice the size and probable age of the different children – what does this tell you about the school and the way in which it was divided into different classes? Notice the children's clothes – what do you learn from these about clothing at the time the photograph was taken? What do you learn about school rules? Notice that no-one was smiling. Does this mean that all these children (and their teacher) disliked being at school and had nothing to smile about? Almost certainly not, but what does it show? One of the further activities at the end of this chapter (number 8) asks you to study old photographs and other school mementoes. The purpose is to identify both the similarities and the differences between education now and then. You might begin with the photograph on this page, comparing it with any of your own school photographs.

The existence of all these old school photographs is also a reminder of one of the most important changes to have taken place in British education during the last 200 years: the introduction of state schools and the requirement that all children attend these schools for a certain number of years.

Today we take for granted that the state will provide a free education for all children. We also take for granted that attendance at school is compulsory. When we look back at education in the late 18th and early 19th centuries we immediately notice a very different situation: a whole variety of private schools, owned by individuals, charities and religious organisations, but without any involvement on the part of either central or local government. One of the main developments in the 19th century was the change from this system of education to one in which the state had a major part to play. It was a gradual change, which began with the introduction in 1833 of government grants to two religious bodies that provided schools, and ended, in the last quarter of the century, with the creation of state elementary schools at which education was both free and compulsory (except for children being educated elsewhere).

There were many reasons why governments became more closely involved in education. One of the most important was the feeling that education for the masses was necessary in a country that was becoming both more democratic and more industrialised. As Britain became more democratic, with most men (though no women) having the vote, it was felt important that ordinary people should at least be able to read and write.

As Britain also became more industrialised, there was a similar need for skilled workers – to make sure that factories, offices and shops were run efficiently. Education was also felt to be important as a way of making sure that the masses behaved themselves and grew up to be reliable and moral citizens. Assignment 15.1 helps you to find out about schooling at the beginning of the 19th century and encourages you to think about some of the reasons why governments became more and more involved.

In the 20th century the state has continued to make greater provision for education: establishing separate state secondary schools; extending the school leaving age to 14 and then to 15 and then to 16; and financing the creation of many new universities and colleges. Education is now a major industry, on which vast sums of money are spent each year (though never as much as those working within it would like). It has also become a major influence on the lives of the British people, all of whom spend at least eleven years of their life in state-run institutions and some of whom spend many more. Asssignment 15.2 asks you to investigate some of the changes that have taken place in state secondary education during the 20th century.

Assignment 15.1
The education of the poor in early 19th century Britain

This assignment helps you to find answers to these questions:

(i) How were poor children educated in early 19th century Britain?

(ii) Why were people so concerned about educating the poor?

(iii) Why did the government begin to get involved in helping to provide an education for poor children?

In order to investigate these questions you will have to find out information from the sources. You will also need to try to identify the attitudes of the various authors. These attitudes may help to explain why many people were so concerned about educating the poor. They may also help to explain why the government eventually became involved in education.

Source A Children at a Dame school

Source B

From a report by the Committee of the Manchester Statistical Society, 1834. This section of the report refers to Dame schools.

The greater part of them are kept by females, but some by old men whose only qualification for this employment seems to be their unfitness for every other. Many of these teachers are engaged at the same time in other employments, such as shopkeeping, sewing, washing, etc. which renders any regular instruction among the scholars absolutely impossible. Indeed neither parents nor teachers seem to consider this as the principal object in sending their children to these schools, but generally say that they go there to be taken care of and to be out of the way at home.

These schools are generally found in very dirty unwholesome rooms – frequently in close damp cellars, or old dilapidated garrets.

Source C

From a report by the Committee of the Manchester Statistical Society, 1834. This section of the report refers to the Common Day Schools.

(These) are in rather better condition but are still very little fitted to give a really useful education to the children of the lower classes. The masters are generally in no way qualified for their occupation, take little interest in it, and show very little inclination or disposition to adopt any of the improvements that have elsewhere been made in the system of instruction. The **terms** are generally low; and it is no uncommon thing to find the master professing to regulate his exertions by the rate of payment he receives from his pupils – that he gives enough for 4d., 6d. or 8d. a week, but that if the scholars would pay higher he would teach them more.

terms: school fees

Source D

VII THAT Bibles and other necessary Books be provided for the Scholars and be paid for by the Treasurer, out of the Subscription.

VIII THAT Objects of this Charity be poor Persons of each Sex, and of any Age above seven Years, who shall be taught to read on Sundays at such Places as shall be appointed by the Committee.

X THAT when more Children apply than can be admitted, the oldest, and those who are at work the rest of the Week, shall have the preference.

XI THAT none shall be refused on account of their Religion, Birth or Settlement provided they reside in the Parish.

XIII THAT Morning and Evening prayers shall be read in each School on every Sunday, by the Teachers or Visitors.

XIV THAT the Teacher and Scholars attend Divine Service on the Morning and Afternoon of every Sunday, except when the Visitor dispense with such attendance.

XV THAT the Teachers shall take care that the Scholars come clean to School; and if any Scholar be guilty of lying, swearing, pilfering, talking indecently or otherwise misbehaving himself, the Teacher shall point out the evil of such Conduct, and if, after repeated reproof, the scholar be not reformed he or she shall be expelled from the School.

Source E

From Joseph Lancaster's *Improvements in Education*, published in 1803

My school is attended by 300 scholars. The whole system of tuition is almost entirely conducted by boys ... The school is divided into classes, to each of these a lad is appointed as monitor: he is responsible for the morals, improvement, good order, and cleanliness of the whole class. It is his duty to make a daily, weekly, and monthly report of progress, specifying the number of lessons performed, boys present, absent etc. etc.

Source F A Board school in the East End of London, 1839

Source G
From the rules of the National School, Kennington, London, 1824

> (The purpose of the school is) to confer upon the Children of the Poor the **Inestimable** Benefit of Religious Instruction, combined with such other Acquirements as may be suitable to their Stations in Life, and calculated to render them useful and respectable Members of Society.
>
> **Inestimable**: so great that it is difficult to estimate

Source H

No. 14.

Northampton Lancasterian School Reading Lessons.

OF THE POOR.

Q. What saith Solomon[a] of oppressing[b] the poor?

A. He that oppresseth the poor reproacheth[c] his Maker: but he that honoureth him hath mercy on the poor.---Rob not the poor, because he is poor, neither oppress[d] the afflicted in the gate,---For the Lord will plead[e] their cause, and spoil the soul of those that spoiled them. Proverbs, c. 14. v. 31. c. 22. v. 22. 23.

Q. Ought we to have pity and compassion on the poor?

A. He that hath pity on the poor, lendeth unto the Lord; and that which he hath given will he pay him again.---He that hath a bountiful eye shall be blessed; for he giveth of his bread to the poor. Proverbs, c. 19. v. 17. c. 22. v. 9.

Source I

From a statement by Lord Brougham, Lord Chancellor, to a parliamentary committee of enquiry, 1834

Do you think that a system of primary education, established by law, would be beneficial?

Brougham: I think that it is wholly inapplicable to the present condition of the country ... Those who recommend it on account of its successful adoption on the Continent, do not reflect upon the funds which it would require and upon the exertions already made in this country by individual **beneficence** ... if the State were to interfere, and obliged every parish to support a school or schools sufficient for educating all children, two consequences would inevitably follow; the greater part of the funds now raised voluntarily for this purpose would be withdrawn and the State or the rate-payers in each parish would have to provide schools for 2,000,000 of children ... a surer way to make education unpopular, and thus **arrest** its progress, could not be devised, than making it the cause either of a general tax, or of an increase in the parish rate.

beneficence: generosity
arrest: stop

Activities

1 Divide a double page into three sections and put one of questions (i) to (iii) on p. 117 at the top of each section. As you read and look at the sources, jot down any points that you think might help you to answer each of these questions. Refer to your notes when answering the questions below.

2 Study the sources. Which different types of school are mentioned in these sources? In each case identify the particular source (or sources) from which you have obtained your information.

3 What do you learn from the written sources about the reasons why these different types of school had been set up? Refer to the sources in detail in support of your answer.

4 What do you learn from these sources about the methods used in educating poor children at this time? In what ways are the methods used by the various types of school (a) similar and (b) different?

5 In the mid-19th century more and more people came to feel that the government should give financial support to elementary education. Using both the sources and your background knowledge, suggest reasons why people might have come to adopt this view?

6 What do you learn from Source I about the reasons why some people objected to the government becoming more closely involved in education? Explain in your own words.

Assignment 15.2
How secondary education developed in 20th century Britain

The Education Act of 1870 led to the introduction in England and Wales of a system of elementary (or primary) education financed and organised by the state. Building on these foundations, governments in the 20th century have gone on to develop a system of state-supported secondary education. In 1902 the Balfour Education Act established local education authorities all over the country. These LEAs, as they came to be called, were given the power to establish secondary schools within their area. LEAs took over control of many existing grammar schools and also set about building new ones. Most pupils at these schools continued to pay fees, though some free places were reserved for children from elementary schools who had passed the 'free place' examination.

During the inter-war years many children continued to receive all of their education at elementary schools, even though the compulsory school leaving age had been raised to 14 by the Fisher Education Act of 1918. A number of government reports recommended that all children should receive a separate secondary education from the age of eleven. These were not fully implemented, however, until the Butler Education Act of 1944. This very important measure required LEAs to provide separate secondary schools for all children and to do so without any charge. Children were to sit an 'eleven plus' examination in order to decide which of three types of school they were to attend: secondary modern schools, technical schools or grammar schools. Education at these three types of school would be geared to the needs of the three different 'types' of child. This system of separated schooling led to much criticism during the 1950s, as a result of which more and more authorities began to abandon the '11+' and to establish instead comprehensive schools attended by all children of secondary age.

The purpose of this assignment is to enable you to see how different kinds of primary evidence can be used to explain the development of secondary education in Britain during these years.

Source A

Bedford School. The buildings in the photograph were erected in 1891 as new premises for an existing grammar school.

Source B

Plan of Bedford School, 1891 (C = classroom)

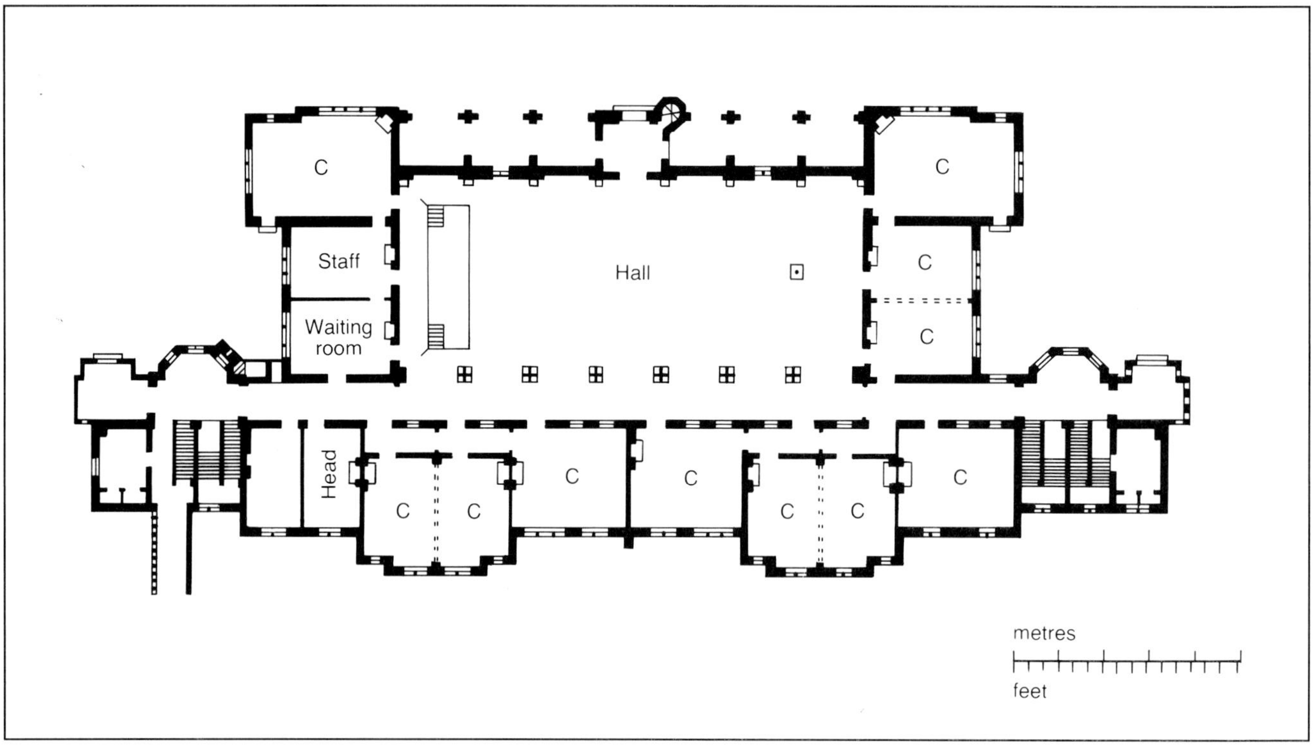

Source C

Plan of Bushbury Secondary Modern School, Wolverhampton, 1949

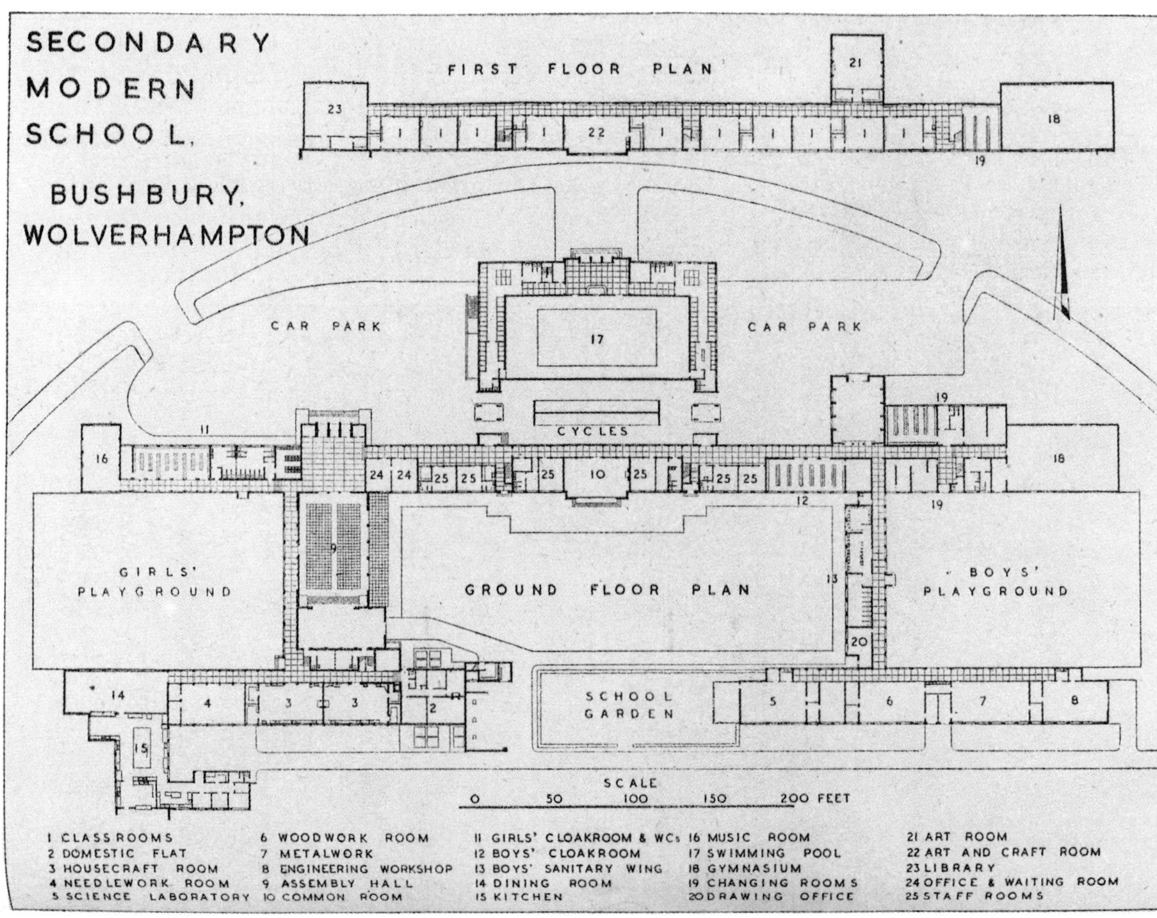

Source D

Plan of Countesthorpe College, Leicestershire. This comprehensive community school was opened in 1970

COMMUNAL (PE, DRAMA, MUSIC)

1 main entrance
2 foyer and dining area
3 coffee and dining area
4 gym store
5 staff changing
6 girls' changing
7 boys' changing
8 tutor
9 switch room
10 caretaker
11 kitchen yard
12 store
13 servery and chair store
14 kitchen
15 staff dining
16 wash-up
17 drama area and theatre
18 drama workshops
19 county players' store
20 music court
21 gramophone room
22 library
23 music room
24 practice room
25 instrument store
26 gymnasium
27 games and PE area
28 PE store
B boys' lavatories
G girls' lavatories
M male staff lavatories
F female staff lavatories

6TH FORM CENTRE, ADMIN

29 enquiries
30 general office
31 cleaner
32 seminar rooms
33 carrels
34 boiler house
35 director of community work area
36 study
37 remedial
38 adult and 6th year cafeteria/social
39 coffee bar
40 community tutors
41 youth and general social area
42 reception
43 drying room
44 covered way

DESIGN CENTRE

45 home economics
46 bedsitting room
47 bath
48 ceramics area
49 ceramics and modelling
50 dress designing
51 general arts, related arts/crafts area
52 woodwork
53 head of department
54 wood machine shop
55 silversmithing
56 staff withdrawal room
57 general practical area
58 covered work area
59 forge area
60 engineering machine shop
61 metalwork
62 engineering project area

MATHS, SCIENCE

63 physics laboratory
64 chemistry preparation
65 demonstration rooms
66 preparation and store
67 planning room
68 general practical laboratory science area
69 general laboratory
70 electronics laboratory
71 animal room
72 biology laboratory
73 drawing office
74 maths
75 maths open plan area
76 staff room
77 language rooms and laboratory
78 recording room
79 a/v technician and store
80 biology pool

LIBRARY, HUMANITIES

81 staff marking
82 general open plan
83 general rooms
84 resource area
85 resources control
86 medical and rest room
87 waiting
88 registrar
89 lecture theatre
90 administration and interview rooms
91 green room
92 biology pool

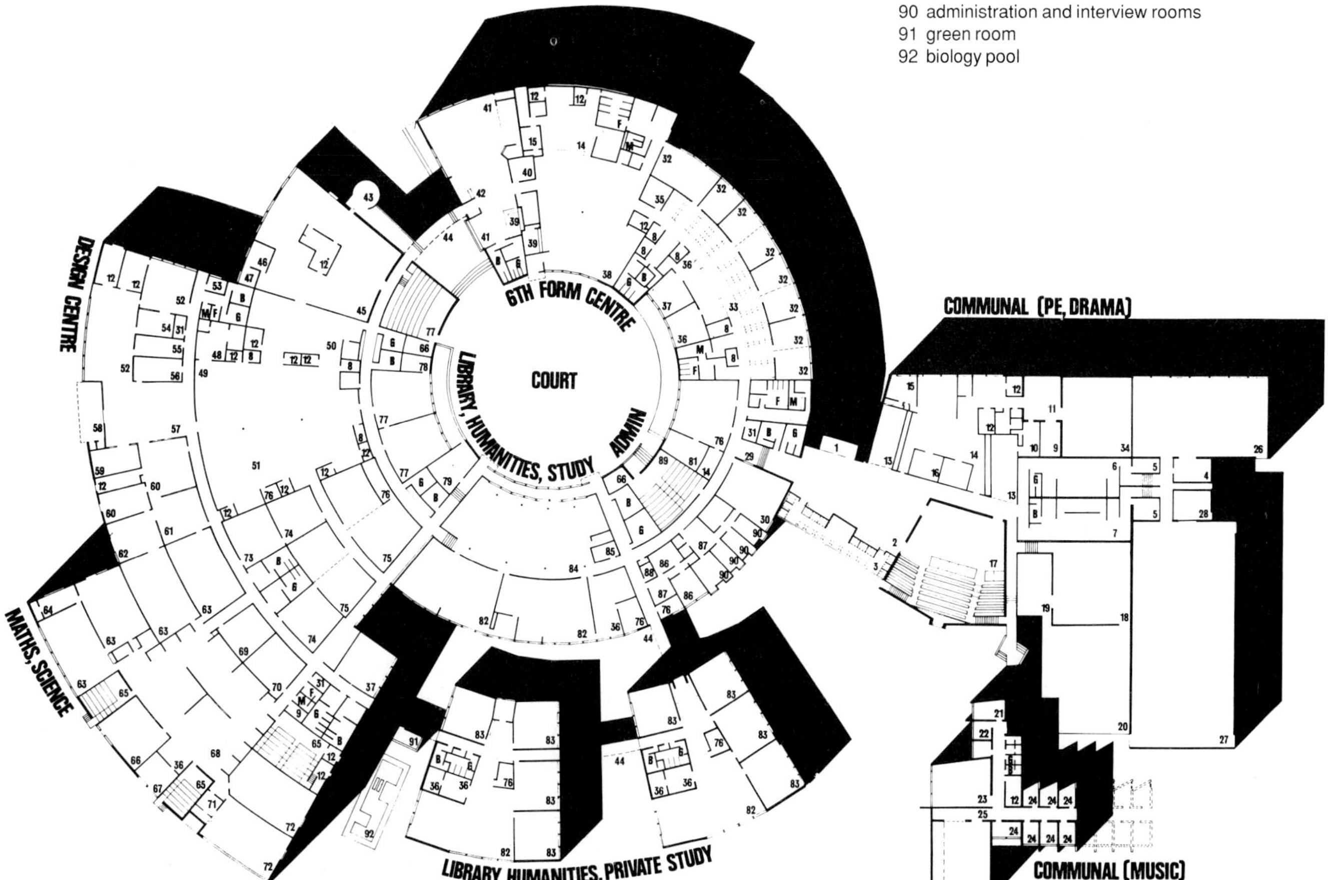

Source E
From the *Regulations for Secondary Schools*, issued by the Board of Education in 1904

4 The Course should provide for instruction in the English Language and Literature, at least one Language other than English, Geography, History, Mathematics, Science and Drawing, with due provision for Manual Work and Physical Exercises, and, in a girls' school, for Housewifery. Not less than 4½ hours per week must be allotted to English, Geography and History; not less than 3½ hours to the Language where only one is taken or less than 6 hours where two are taken; and not less than 7½ hours to Science and Mathematics, of which at least three must be for Science. The instruction in Science must be both theoretical and practical. Where two languages other than English are taken, and Latin is not one of them, the Board will require to be satisfied that the omission of Latin is for the advantage of the school.

5 In a girls' school in which the total number of hours of instruction is less than 22 per week, the time given to Science and Mathematics may be reduced to one third of that total, provided that at least three hours are given to Science.

Source F
From *The New Secondary Education*, a pamphlet issued by the Ministry of Education in 1947

Perhaps the main difference between a modern school and other types of secondary schools is its very broad outlook and objective. It has to provide a series of courses for children of widely differing ability, aptitude and social background. It has to cater for the needs of intelligent boys and girls, for those with a marked practical bent, as well as for the special problem of backward children.

The aim of the modern school is to provide a good all-round secondary education, not focused primarily on the traditional subjects of the school curriculum, but developing out of the interests of the children. Through its appeal to their interests it will stimulate their ability to learn and will teach them to pursue quality in thought, expression and craftsmanship. It will interpret the modern world to them and give them a preparation for life in the widest sense, including a full use of leisure. It will aim at getting the most out of every pupil that he is capable of, at making him adaptable, and at teaching him to do a job properly and thoroughly and not to be satisfied with bad workmanship, and to be exact in what he says and does. Freedom and flexibility are of its essence and are indeed its great opportunity.

Source G
From *What is a Comprehensive School?* by Margaret Cole, a pamphlet issued by the London Labour Party in 1954

The idea of a comprehensive high school is that it shall cater for all children within a particular area from the age of eleven-plus to the time when they leave school, whether that be at fifteen, sixteen, seventeen, or whenever, except, of course, the handicapped children who need some form of special education, and the minority which will at present continue to go to the various kinds of independent and voluntary schools which still exist. For all the others – the great majority – children of all kinds, when they leave their primary schools, will enter the same high school.

This means that we deny the two assumptions on which most of the secondary education of today is based, that there are three types of child and three only – the grammar child, the technical child, and the modern child, of which the grammar child is the best. Anyone with any practical experience of children knows that both these assumptions are nonsense. There are not three 'types' of child but many types; and what we have to do, if we want to secure that every child receives the kind of education which best fits it for adult life and service to the community, is to see that courses of study are provided in schools which will bring out and develop every child's particular gifts.

Activities

1 What do you learn from Sources A, B, C and D about the kinds of education provided at these three schools? Refer in detail to the sources in support of your answer.

2 What are the strengths and weaknesses of Sources B, C and D as pieces of historical evidence? Refer to the sources in support of your answer.

3 What do you learn from Source E about early 19th century attitudes towards education?

4 Compare Sources C and F. Does Source C suggest that the government's plans for secondary education (as outlined in Source F) were being implemented? Explain your answer.

5 (i) In what ways would the writer of Source G disagree with Source F?

(ii) Does Source D illustrate the kind of school recommended in Source G? Explain your answer.

6 What reasons help to explain the following:

(i) Why governments have made greater provision for secondary education during the twentieth century.

(ii) Why secondary modern and grammar schools were largely replaced by comprehensive schools during the 1960s and 1970s.

Further activities

1 Give an account of the ways in which the children of the upper classes were educated during the second half of the 19th century. In what ways during the 19th century did the education of such children (a) change and (b) remain the same?

2 As someone trying to find out about Victorian Britain, give reasons why it is important to study education in Victorian times.

3 Try to get hold of the 1851 Education Census for your area. What do you learn from this census about (a) the different types of school in your area and (b) the extent to which the poor were receiving an education at that time? How would you explain your findings?

4 Using your own classroom, try to recreate what would have happened in an early 19th century monitorial school. What, if anything, do you learn from this re-creation about the effects of the monitorial system?

5 Many modern primary schools began as Board schools established as a result of the Education Act of 1870. Find one of these schools in your area and study the log book kept by teachers at the school at the end of the 19th century. What do you learn from the log book about; (a) the way the school was divided into different classes; (b) the size of classes; (c) teaching methods; (d) how education at the school changed during the period you are studying; (e) the way of life of local people; and (f) the strengths and weaknesses of log books as historical evidence?

6 Ask older relatives to let you study any mementoes they may have of their own schooldays (a 'memento' is something that people keep to remind themselves of their own past). These mementoes might include old school photographs, magazines, textbooks, reports, certificates, exercise books. What do you learn from this evidence about the ways in which education now and then is both (a) different and (b) similar? How would you try to explain both the differences and the similarities?

16 *Medicine and Health*

This is how one patient in the early 19th century described his feelings about having an operation:

> *A patient preparing for an operation was like a condemned criminal preparing for an execution. He counted the days till the appointed day came. He counted the hours of the day till the appointed hour came. He listened for the echo in the street of the surgeon's carriage. He watched for his pull at the door bell; for his foot on the stair; for his step in the room; for the production of his dreaded instruments; for his few grave words, and his last preparations before beginning. And then he surrendered his liberty, revolting at the necessity, submitting to be held and bound, and helplessly gave himself up to the cruel knife.*

Look at where the operation took place. Think what this tells you about how it was conducted. Notice how the patient remained conscious throughout. Then compare this account with what you know about surgery today. This should give you some idea of the extent to which medical practice has changed over the last 200 years. In studying the history of medicine and health during this period the purpose is to try to find out why these changes have occurred and the effects they have had. This chapter looks at two aspects of the history of medicine: changes in medical knowledge and changes in the ways in which medical services are provided. Assignment 16.1 examines the introduction of anaesthesia during the mid-19th century, a development that revolutionised surgery. Assignment 16.2 looks at the creation of the National Health Service after the Second World War, a development that brought about a similar revolution in the provision of medical care.

An operation at Charing Cross Hospital, late 19th century

Assignment 16.1
James Simpson and the introduction of chloroform

Before the 1840s operations were performed in the way described at the beginning of this chapter. The only way of relieving the agony was by administering drugs such as alcohol or laudanum. These may have dulled the sensation of pain, but were clearly unable to render the patient unconscious. In the 1840s ether was first used in operations in the United States and was soon introduced into Britain, the first recorded instance being its use by Robert Liston during an operation to amputate a leg in 1846.

One doctor who was quick to see the advantages of anaesthesia was James Simpson, Professor of Midwifery at the University of Edinburgh, at that time one of the greatest medical centres in Europe. Midwifery in the past had been a rather neglected area of medicine and Simpson had worked hard to give it a higher status within the medical world. He was particularly concerned at the extent of some women's sufferings during childbirth (At this time, in addition, many women experienced a very large number of pregnancies). He used ether very successfully, but found that it had a number of problems. He therefore began to experiment with possible substitutes.

This assignment looks at Simpson's discovery of the use of chloroform. It is particularly concerned with the controversy that subsequently developed as to whether or not chloroform should be administered during childbirth. This was a question about which many people felt very strongly during the 1840s and 1850s. As often with medical controversies, the differences of opinion tell us a great deal about the general attitudes of the time.

Source A
From James Miller, *The Principles of Surgery,* Philadelphia, 1852

Late one evening – it was the 4th of November, 1847 – on returning home after a weary day's labour, Dr Simpson, with his two friends and assistants, Drs Keith and Matthew Duncan, sat down to their somewhat hazardous work in Dr Simpson's dining room. Having inhaled several substances, but without much effect, it occurred to Dr Simpson to try a **ponderous** material, which he had formerly set aside on a ... table, and which, on account of its great weight, he had hitherto regarded as of no likelihood whatever. That happened to be a small bottle of chloroform. It was searched for, and recovered from beneath a heap of waste paper. And with each tumbler newly charged, the inhalers resumed their (task). Immediately an **unwonted hilarity** seized the party; they become bright-eyed, very happy and very **loquacious** ... The conversation was of unusual intelligence, and quite charmed the listeners – some ladies of the family and a naval officer, brother-in-law of Dr Simpson. But suddenly there was talk of sounds being heard like those of a cotton mill, louder and louder; a moment more, then all was quiet, and then – a crash ... On awaking, Dr Simpson's first (thought) was "This is far stronger and better than ether" ...

ponderous: heavy
unwonted hilarity: joking and laughing that was unexpected
loquacious: talkative

Source B

An extract from a pamphlet written by James Simpson *(Account of a new Anaesthetic Agent as a Substitute for Sulphuric Ether in Surgery and Midwifery, 1847)* in which he argued that chloroform was preferable to ether for four reasons

1 A greatly less quantity of Chloroform ... is requisite to produce the anaesthetic effect ...

2 Its action is much more rapid and complete, and generally more persistent ...

3 Most of those who know ... the sensations produced by Ether inhalation, and those who have subsequently breathed the Chloroform, have strongly declared the inhalation and influence of Chloroform to be far more agreeable and pleasant than those of Ether ...

4 I believe that, considering the small quantity requisite, as compared with Ether, the use of Chloroform will be less expensive ...

requisite: needed

Source C

From a contemporary doctor's account of one woman's condition during childbirth.(Letter from Dr Henry Bennet in the medical journal *Lancet*, 1848.) The writer practised in London.

... the head (of the baby) advanced and receded slightly ... at each pain; the vagina was dry and of a stinging heat; the pains were slight, occurring every two minutes, and apparently cut short by the screams and disordered efforts and motions of the patient. The latter was in a state of frantic agitation, screaming and plunging in every direction as soon as the pains came on ... The skin was hot and dry; the pulse full, 120; the eyes bloodshot ...; the tongue white, but moist. Had chloroform not been available I should certainly have felt myself called upon to take fifteen or twenty ounces of blood from the arm, in order to remove the general congestion, and to allay the irritability of the nervous system.

Source D

A contemporary illustration of a portable chloroform inhaler developed by Dr J Snow in the late 1840s. English doctors administered chloroform by means of inhalers whereas Simpson and other Scottish doctors applied it on a cloth or handkerchief.

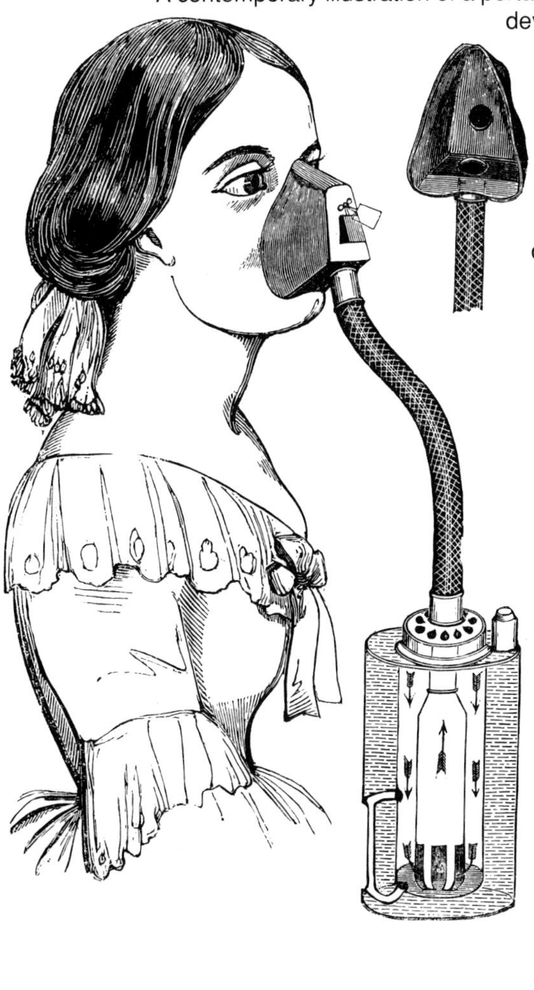

Source E

A further extract from the pamphlet by James Simpson quoted in Source B

All of us, I most sincerely believe, are called upon to employ it (anaesthesia) by every principle of true humanity, as well as by every principle of true religion. Medical men may oppose (the use of anaesthesia in labour), but they will oppose it in vain; for certainly our patients themselves will force the use of it upon the profession ... Medical men will, no doubt, ... insist on mothers continuing to endure, in all their primitive intensity, all the agonies of childbirth, as a proper sacrifice to the ... doctrine of the desirability of pain.

Source F

From a comment by a religious writer on the use of chloroform in childbirth, late 1840s

> *pain ... may be considered even as a blessing of the Gospel, and being a blessing, admits of being met well or ill.*

Source G

From Denman's *Introduction to the Practice of Midwifery*, first published in 1782, and quoted by Dr G.T. Gream in an article in the *Lancet* in 1849 opposing the use of anaesthesia in childbirth

> ... in everything which relates to the act of **parturition,** Nature ... is fully competent to accomplish her own purpose; she may be truly said to ... **abhor** assistance ... all women should believe, and find comfort in the reflection, that they are at those times under the peculiar care of **Providence**, and that their safety in child-birth is ensured by more numerous and powerful resources than under any other circumstances ...
>
> **parturition**: childbirth
> **abhor**: hate
> **Providence:** God

Activities

1 Study Source A.

(i) What questions would you need to ask before deciding whether or not this is an accurate account of the events to which it refers?

(ii) Compare Simpson's researches into anaesthesia with what you know of the methods used by medical researchers today. What do you notice about the differences between these methods and how would you explain them?

2 Study Source B. Is Simpson likely to have thought that one of these advantages of chloroform was more important than the others? Explain your answer.

3 'Conservative doctors strongly opposed the use of anaesthesia in childbirth.' Does Source C support this statement? Give reasons for your answer.

4 Do Sources C and D suggest that medicine in London was more advanced than that in Edinburgh? Explain your answer.

5 Sources E, F and G all refer to religion. Do they do so in similar ways? Give reasons for your answer.

6 Do you learn anything from these sources about (a) attitudes towards women and (b) the position of women in society? Explain your answer.

Assignment 16.2
Aneurin Bevan, the doctors and the NHS

One of the most important developments in 20th century Britain has been the way in which the state has become increasingly involved in providing welfare services for its citizens. Two periods stand out as those during which the foundations of the modern welfare state were laid: the reforming Liberal governments of 1906–14 and the post-war Labour governments of 1945–51. This assignment examines one of the most important welfare measures of the latter period: the creation of the National Health Service (NHS).

One of the recommendations of the Beveridge Report of 1942 (see Assignment 14.2) had been 'the provision of a free national health service to everybody'. Detailed proposals for what this might involve were included in a government report (or White Paper) issued in 1944. With the election of a Labour government in 1945 it became the responsibility of Aneurin Bevan, the new Minister of Health, to turn these proposals into reality. It was no easy task – above all because of the opposition of part of the medical profession, led by the British Medical Association (BMA), the professional body representing doctors' interests. Although the National Health Service Bill was approved by parliament in 1946, it did not come into operation until 1948. In the meantime Bevan had a hard job convincing many doctors that they should join the new NHS. The purpose of this assignment is to study some of the evidence that relates to this struggle between Bevan and the BMA and to identify the problems that might arise in trying to use this evidence.

Source A

From Aneurin Bevan's speech in the House of Commons debate on the National Health Service Bill, 30 April 1946

In the last two years there has been such a clamour from **sectional interests** in the field of national health that we are in danger of forgetting why these proposals are brought forward ... The first reason why a health scheme of this sort is necessary at all is because it has been the firm conclusion of all parties that money ought not to be permitted to stand in the way of obtaining an efficient health service. Although it is true that the national health insurance system provides a general practitioner service and caters for something like 21 million of the population, the rest of the population have to pay whenever they desire the services of a doctor ... and therefore tend to postpone consultation as long as possible (while) there is the financial anxiety caused by having to pay doctors' bills ... Furthermore, it gives no backing to the doctor in the form of specialist services ... Our hospital organisation has grown up with no plan, with no system; it is unevenly distributed over the country and indeed it is one of the tragedies of the situation that very often the best hospital facilities are available where they are least needed ... One of the first merits of this Bill is that it provides a universal health service without any insurance qualifications of any sort. It is available to the whole population and ... it is intended that there shall be no limitation on the kind of assistance given – the general practitioner service, the specialist, the hospitals, eye treatment, spectacles, dental treatment, hearing facilities, all of these are to be made available free.

sectional interests: groups of people anxious to look after their own interests

Source B

From the results of a questionnaire sent out to doctors by the BMA in 1944.

Doctors were asked to comment on the proposals of the 1944 White Paper, *A National Health Service*. The figures are all in percentages. 'Service doctors' are those serving at the time in the armed forces. 'Consultants' are senior doctors, mostly working in hospitals. 'Salaried doctors' were mainly people employed in administration.

Source C

From Bevan's memoirs, *In Place of Fear*, published in 1952

I usually met (the BMA's) representatives when they had come hot from a conference at which the wildest speeches had been made. My trade union experiences had taught me to distinguish between the atmosphere of the mass demonstration and the quite different mood of the negotiating table. I was therefore able to discount a great deal of what had been said (at the conference).

Source D

From a letter in the *British Medical Journal*, 1946, by Dr Alfred Cox, a leading doctor actively involved in the BMA

I have examined the Bill (the 1946 National Health Service Bill) and it looks uncommonly like the first step, and a big one, towards National Socialism (Nazism) as practised in Germany. The medical service there was early put under the dictatorship of a "Medical Fuehrer". This Bill will establish the Minister of Health in that capacity.

Source E

From a speech by a doctor at a public meeting in Wimbledon Town Hall, 1946

... (the nationalisation of hospitals) is the greatest seizure of property since Henry VIII confiscated the monasteries.

Source F

A cartoon by David Low, published 15 January 1948. The figure shown dreaming represents the BMA. The figure on the operating table represents Bevan.

OPERATION SABOTAGE

Activities

1 Study Source A.

(i) What, according to Bevan, were the purposes of the National Health Service Bill?

(ii) Using both Source A and your textbooks, show how this Bill tried to achieve these purposes.

(iii) Does Bevan indicate in this speech that the bill had proved very controversial? Refer to the source in support of your answer.

2 The BMA was strongly opposed to the 1944 White Paper and to many of the arrangements for the proposed NHS. Does Source B show that most doctors supported their stand on this issue?

3 Referring to Source B, explain why some doctors considered more favourably than others the idea of a national health service.

4 How reliable are Sources C, D, E and F as evidence for the attitudes of doctors towards the introduction of a national health service? Refer in detail to the sources in support of your answer.

5 'Cartoons usually tell us more about the cartoonist than about the events to which they refer.' Do you agree? Illustrate your answer by reference to Source F.

Further activities

1 Make a list of remedies for disease used during the 18th century. What do these remedies tell you about people's beliefs concerning the causes of disease?

2 Try to get hold of a family health book or popular medical encyclopaedia published before 1945. Read what it has to say about childbirth. Compare this with the advice that is given in a book published recently. What differences do you notice and how might you explain them?

3 Choose *one* of the following diseases: pneumonia; tuberculosis; polio; diphtheria. Describe how the treatment of this disease has changed during the last 100 years. How would you explain the changes that you have identified?

4 Interview *two* people about their experiences of health care before and after the introduction of the NHS in 1948. What do you learn from these interviews about the impact of the NHS?

5 Choose *two* medical questions about which people today frequently disagree on moral grounds, e.g. abortion or genetic engineering. Give the arguments for and against. Why do you think people have often disagreed very strongly about medical questions such as these?

17 *Religion*

Look at the textbook (or textbooks) that you are using for British social history. How much is there on religion? Probably very little – perhaps nothing at all. Stop for a moment to think why this is. It isn't because religion was unimportant in 18th and 19th century Britain. As you will find out from this chapter, it was very important indeed. The people who wrote your textbooks and planned your GCSE syllabuses live in a society where religion is much less important than it used to be. Their choice of topics probably tells you more about *them* than it does about the periods you are studying. This often happens in history when people look back from one age to another. They see the past very much from their own point of view.

In some ways the fact that Britain was a Christian country in the 18th century is just as important as the fact that it was experiencing an industrial revolution. Almost everyone in the 18th century accepted the truth of Christianity without thinking to question it – and this was probably true even of those who did not go to church. In England the Church of England was a very powerful organisation which exerted a great deal of influence over people in all walks of life. Even during the 19th century, when religious belief came under increasing attack, religion continued to be central to the life of the country. More books were published on religious subjects than on anything else. When he was Prime Minister in the last quarter of the 19th century Gladstone often spent as much time worrying about the appointment of bishops – events that are never mentioned in textbooks – as about all the famous acts of parliament associated with his name.

In the 18th century most English people were Anglicans, i.e. they belonged to the Church of England. During the second half of the 18th century and the first half of the 19th century, however, there was a big increase in the number of people attending other churches, both Protestant Nonconformist (e.g. Methodist, Baptist and Presbyterian) and Roman Catholic. Partly because of this, the mid-19th century was a period of great religious conflict: between Anglicans and Nonconformists, between Roman Catholics and Protestants, and even within the Church of England itself. This conflict was another sign that religion was taken very seriously. There were a number of attempts to disestablish the Church of England, i.e. to remove state support for the Church of England and to make it like any of the other churches. All these attempts failed.

The first assignment (17.1) in this chapter examines one of the first challenges to the Church of England during the 18th century – the rise of Methodism. Its purpose is to look at the long-term consequences of the rise of Methodism and to show how events in the 18th century still have important effects today. The second assignment (17.2) asks the question 'Was Victorian England religious?'. The author of this book has just said that it was, but to what extent is this true?

Assignment 17.1
The impact of Methodism

Look at Sources E and F. These show you at a glance that Methodism has had major long-term effects. With 20 million members worldwide it is not surprising that the 250th anniversary of John Wesley's conversion prompted celebrations like the one reported in Source F. Twenty million is a lot of people and the continuing importance of Methodism today is one reason why its history is worth studying. In the short term, in the 18th and 19th centuries, it was also a major influence on British life. It is difficult to understand British social history during that period without some understanding of the Methodist movement. The purpose of this assignment is to examine both its short-term and its long-term effects.

John Wesley (1703–91), the founder of Methodism, was an Anglican clergyman who had no desire to break away from the church of which he was a member. In 1738 he underwent a deep spiritual experience which led him to believe that Christ had saved him. The purpose of his life from then on was to persuade others to turn to Christ and thus to experience salvation for themselves as well. There was nothing very new about what Wesley was saying. This, after all, was what Christians down the ages had often said. It was Wesley's enthusiasm that was so special. He was also determined that his message should reach everyone, however poor and humble.

The Church of England gave Wesley little encouragement. He turned instead to preaching out of doors, especially in parts of the country where the Church of England had made little attempt to reach the masses. Eventually Wesley was forced to organise a church of his own and 'Wesleyan' chapels began to spring up all over the country. By 1815 there were a quarter of a million Methodists in Britain and approximately the same number in the United States (which for most of Wesley's lifetime had been still under British rule).

Source A

From John Gay, *The Geography of Religion in England*, 1971

The critical period for the spread of Methodism was from the time of its institution in 1740 right through the 18th century to the early years of the 19th century. It is a strange coincidence that John Wesley began his work just as the population graph started its upward climb and just as industrialisation began in earnest.

Throughout the expanding industrial north and the Black Country the Church of England's **parochial machinery** was unable to cater for the needs of the mushrooming population. Churches were too small, too few, **badly endowed**, badly staffed and unrealistically sited. Nobody could remember when changes had last been made.

... It was (in) the newly industrialised settlements (that) the Church of England was at its weakest and Methodism came in to fill the vacuum ... Methodism was to become most influential in the areas where the Church of England had failed to provide for the **pastoral needs** of the people – in Cornwall, the Black Country, the north-east coast and the new industrial areas in Lancashire and Yorkshire.

parochial machinery: parish system ('parochial' means 'parish')
badly endowed: lacking in money
pastoral needs: the need to be cared for by the Church

Source B
The distribution of Methodists in England in 1851. The map is based on the figures obtained from a national census of church attendance taken in 1851. The 'Index of Attendance' refers to the percentage of the total population attending a Methodist church. The 'Index of Attendance' was calculated on the basis of the total number of attendances at the morning, afternoon and evening services on the day of the census (some people would therefore have been recorded two or three times).

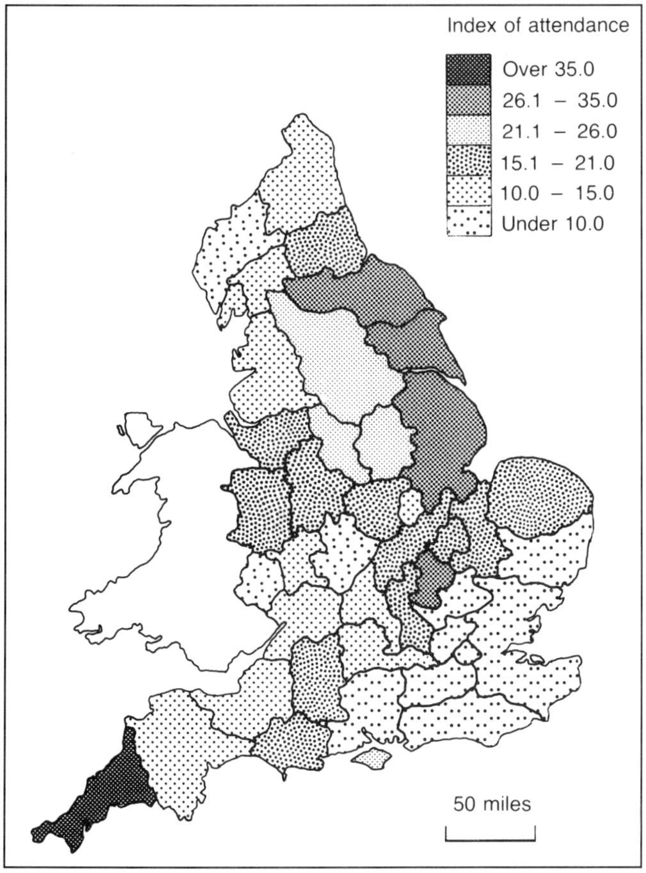

Source C
The distribution of Methodists in England in 1961

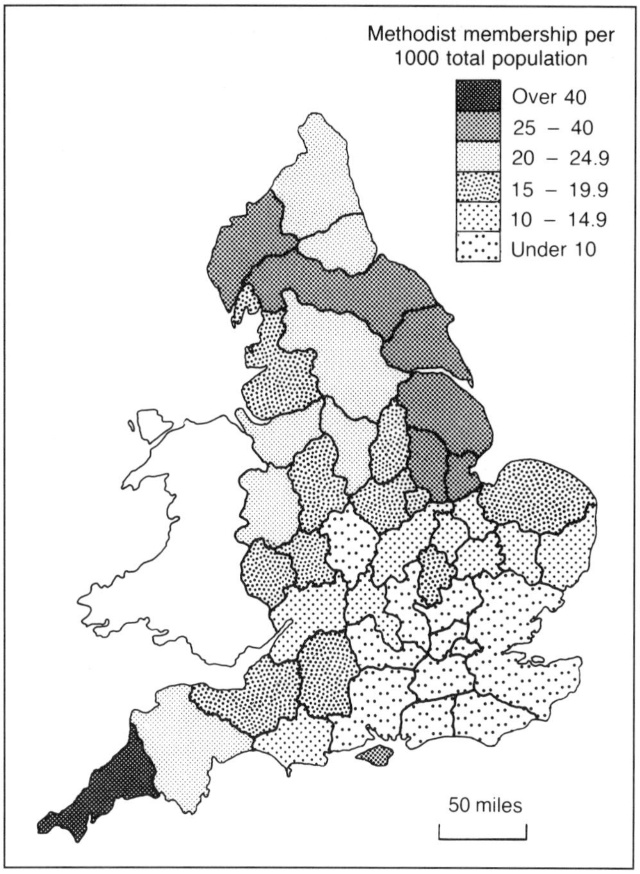

Source D
Gledholt Methodist Church, Huddersfield, Yorkshire, built in 1890

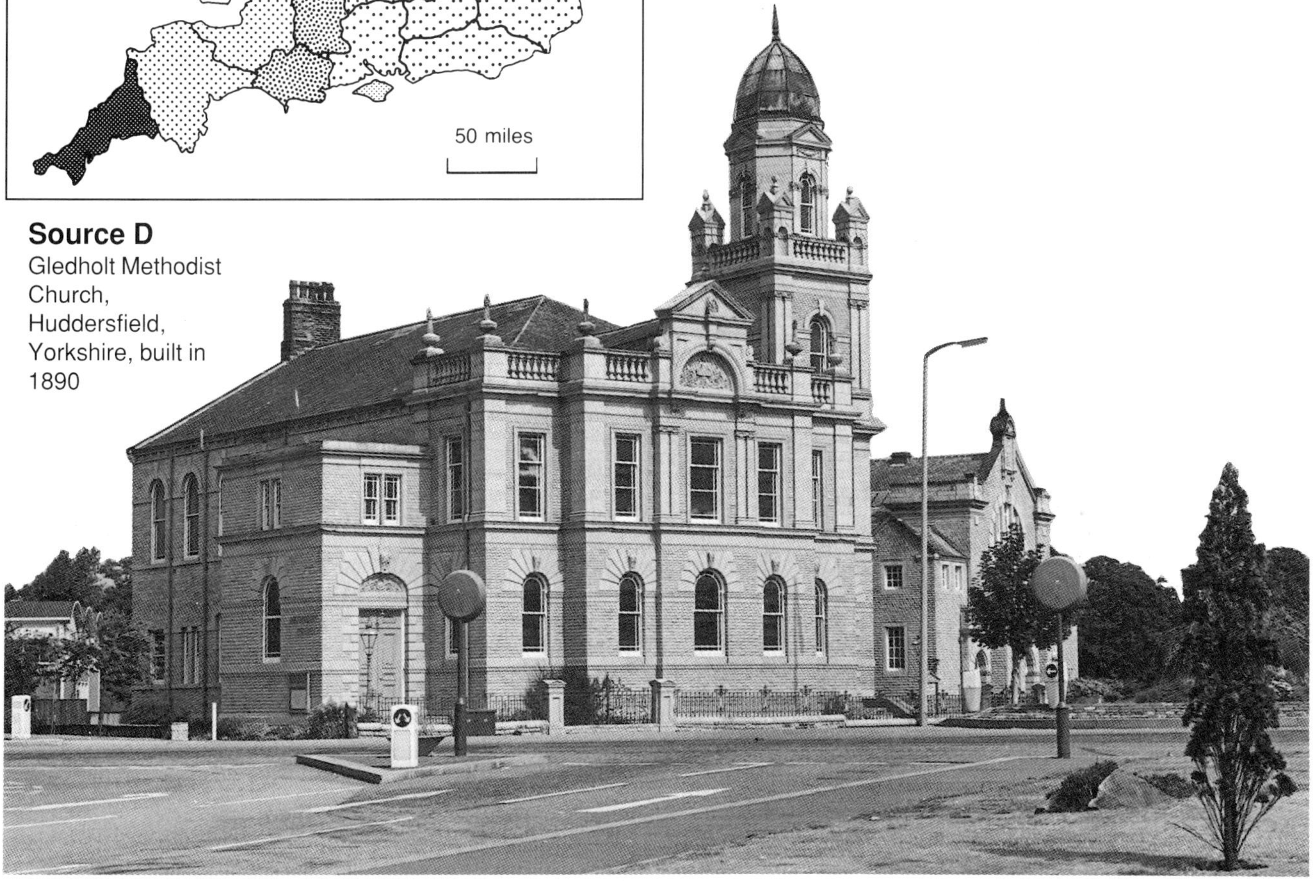

Source E

A map showing the number of Methodists in different parts of the world (from Jim Bates, *The Methodist Church*, 1977). 'Part Methodist' is the estimated number of Methodists in areas of the world where Methodists have joined with other Christian groups to form a united church.

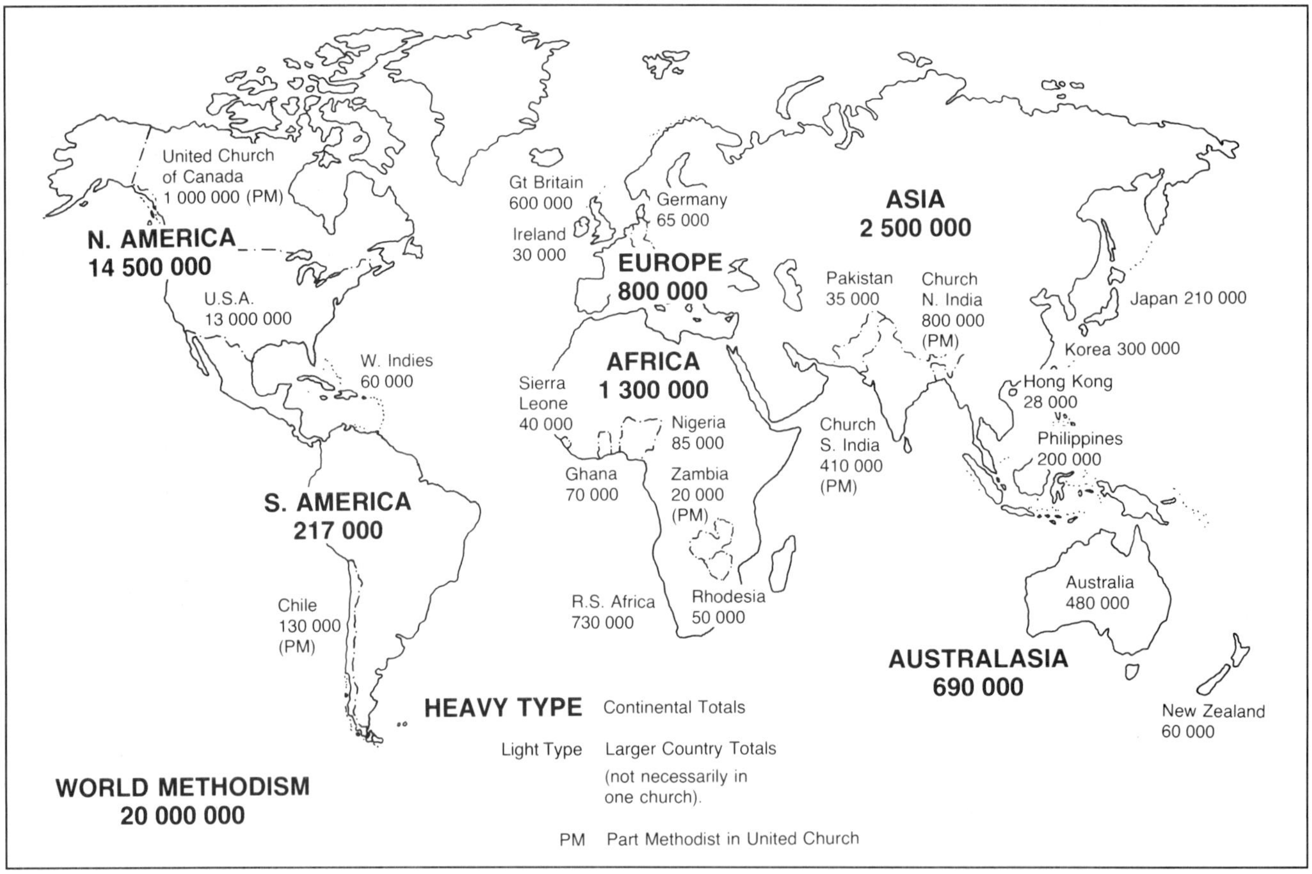

Activities

1 (i) What do you learn from Source A about the reasons for the spread of Methodism?

(ii) Referring to your background knowledge, identify any other reasons that help to explain the spread of Methodism.

2 (i) To what extent does Source B support Source A? Refer in detail to both sources in support of your answer.

(ii) What do you learn from Source B about the impact of Methodism on England during the years to 1850?

3 (i) Why is it difficult to compare Sources B and C?

(ii) What do you learn from Source C about the changes that took place in the position of Methodism between 1851 and 1961?

4 Does Source D tell you anything about the position of Methodism at the end of the 19th century? Explain your answer.

5 Study Source E. Choose three areas of the world (exclude the British Isles) to which Methodism has spread. How would you explain the spread of Methodism to the areas that you have chosen?

6 How does Source F support Source E?

Source F

From *Radio Times*, August 1988

Three presenters – Cliff Michelmore, Sally Magnusson and Roger Royle (right) – on three trains re-create the historic travels of John Wesley. David White hitches a ride

In the tracks of WESLEY

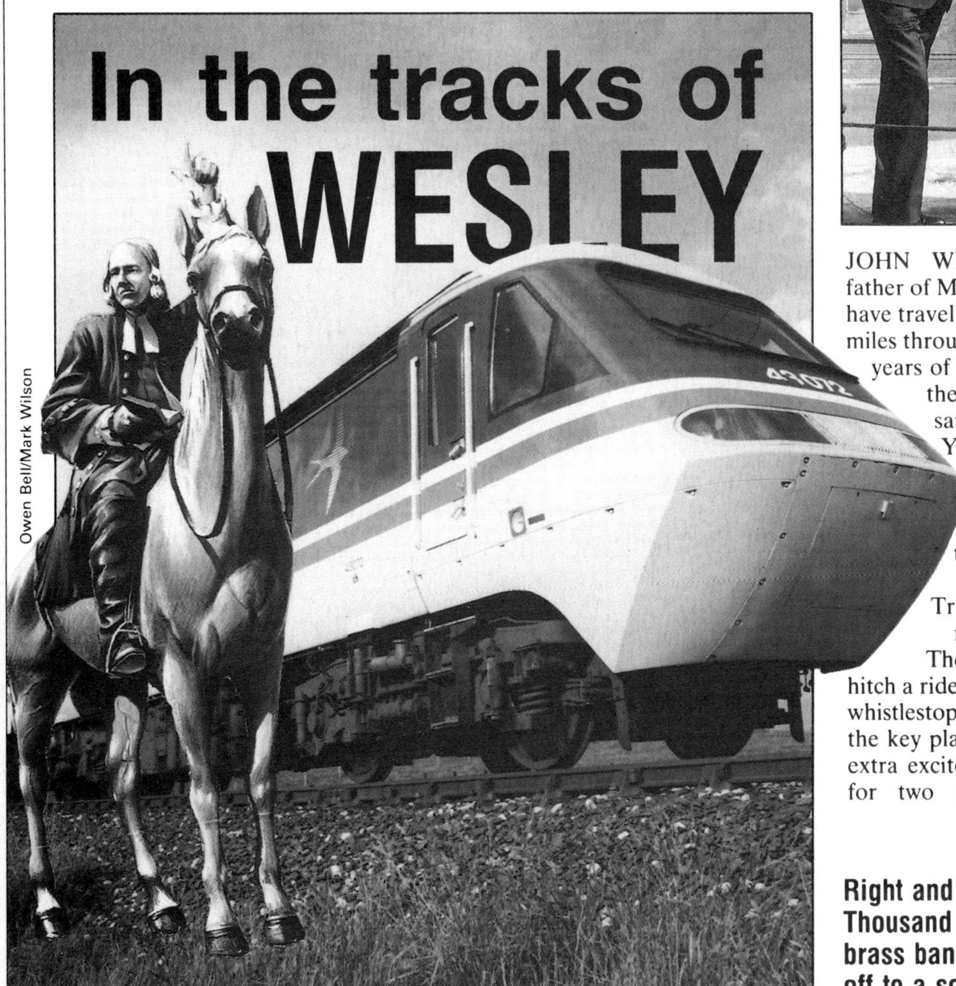

Owen Bell/Mark Wilson

JOHN WESLEY, the founding father of Methodism, is reckoned to have travelled a quarter of a million miles throughout Britain in some 50 years of preaching. 'I look on all the world as my parish,' he said. A hard act to follow. Yet, in the 250th anniversary year of Wesley's conversion, Songs of Praise was determined to do just that – by train (a 125mph High Speed Train covers a quarter of a million miles each year). The programme planned to hitch a ride aboard three trains on a whistlestop pilgrimage to some of the key places of Wesley's life. For extra excitement, it would arrange for two of the trains to run

Right and centre: 'O for a Thousand Tongues . . .' The brass band and choir get things off to a sound start

Assignment 17.2
Was Victorian England religious?

The purpose of this assignment is to look at some of the kinds of evidence that you might use if you were trying to answer the question 'Was Victorian England religious?' In looking at this evidence you will need to do two things: (a) decide how useful each piece of evidence is likely to be to someone trying to answer this question; and (b) come to some conclusion about what you learn from each piece of evidence.

Source A

A map showing attendance at church on Sunday 30 March, 1851, the day of the religious census. The 'Index of Attendance' refers to the percentage of the total population attending church. Remember that the index was calculated on the basis of attendances at the morning, afternoon and evening services. (Some people would therefore have been recorded two or three times – hence the 'over 100%' box on the table).

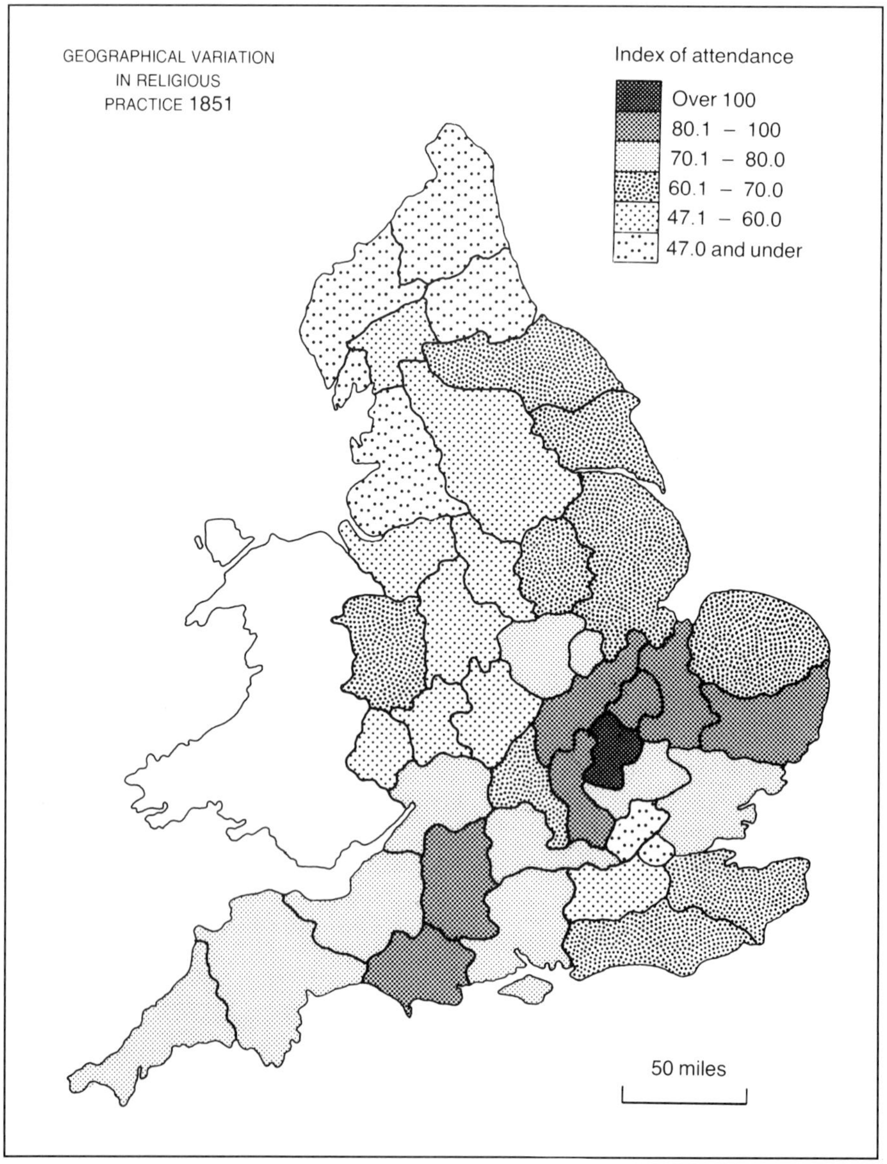

Source B

From the novel *Hard Times* by Charles Dickens, published in 1854. 'Coketown' is the imaginary northern town in which the story of the novel takes place.

You saw nothing in Coketown but what was severely workful. If the members of a **religious persuasion** built a chapel there – as the members of eighteen religious persuasions had done – they made it a **pious** warehouse of red brick, with sometimes ... a bell in a bird-cage on the top of it ...

... the perplexing mystery of the place was, Who belonged to the eighteen **denominations**? Because, whoever did, the labouring people did not. It was very strange to walk through the streets on a Sunday morning, and note how few of them the barbarous jangling of bells ... called away from their own quarter, from their own close rooms, from the corners of their own streets, where they lounged listlessly, gazing at all the church- and chapel-going, as at a thing with which they had no manner of concern.

religious persuasion or denomination: a particular branch of the Christian Church (e.g. Baptist, Methodist, etc.)

pious: religious

Source C

From an account by an Anglican bishop.W. D. Maclagan, *entitled The Church and the People*, published in 1882. The writer was commenting on the rapid growth in the size of English towns earlier in the century.

... it is easy to see how the ... labourer fresh from the country villages where, at least, they might find room, and often sought it, in the House of God, should gradually lose the habit of worship and devotion, where there was neither place for them to worship nor pastor to lead them in the ways of God.

Source D

Comments by a former London costermonger (someone who sells things in the street from a barrow) to the writer Henry Mayhew, published in Mayhew's *London Life and the London Poor*, 1851

Religion is a regular puzzle to the costers. They see people come out of church and chapel, and as they're mostly well-dressed, and there's very few of their own sort among the church-goers, the costers somehow mix up being religious with being respectable, and so they have a queer sort of feeling about it. It's a mystery to them.

Source E

From the memoirs of Francis Galton, a Victorian scientist entitled *Memories of My Life*, published in 1908. The author refers to Darwin's *The Origin of the Species*, a book which put forward the theory of evolution. This theory clashed with the traditional view of the Church, which was that human beings had been specifically created by God.

> *The publication in 1859 of* The Origin of Species *by Charles Darwin (marked a new stage) in my own mental development, as it did in that of human thought generally. Its effect was to demolish (many) barriers by a single stroke, and to arouse a spirit of rebellion against all ancient authorities whose ... statements were contradicted by modern science.*

Activities

1 Study each of the sources in turn, bearing in mind the problem that has been set for this assignment, i.e. 'Was Victorian England religious?'.

How useful are each of these sources to someone trying to answer this question? Refer in detail to the sources, commenting on their strengths and weaknesses as evidence. In the case of each source explain how you might (or might not) use it to answer the question.

2 What do you learn from your background knowledge that might help you to answer this question?

3 Using your answers to Questions 1 and 2, write an essay with the title 'Was Victorian England religious?'

Further activities

1 Choose *one* church or chapel in your local area that was built during the 18th or 19th century. Write a history of this church from its foundation until the present day, concentrating on why it was built and how and why the life of the church has changed.

2 Investigate the part played during the 19th century by churches and clergymen in your local area in (a) education, (b) poor relief and (c) other aspects of social welfare.

3 (i) What do you learn from the religious census of 1851 about church attendance in your area?

(ii) Try to find out about church attendance in your area today.

(iii) How might you explain the differences between church attendance in 1851 and church attendance today?

18 *The Changing Role of Women*

Hearing in 1870 that someone called Lady Amberley had made a speech in favour of votes for women, Queen Victoria wrote the following angry letter to an acquaintance:

> *The Queen is most anxious to enlist everyone who can speak or write or join in checking this mad, wicked folly of "Women's Rights" with all its attendant horrors, on which her poor feeble sex is bent, forgetting every sense of womanly feeling and* ***propriety****. Lady Amberley ought to get a good whipping.*

propriety: sense of what is right or proper

Many British men (and some women) would probably have agreed with Queen Victoria that Lady Amberley deserved 'a good whipping' for speaking in favour of votes for women. Like her they thought of women as the 'poor feeble sex'. Like her they were strongly opposed to equal rights.

Views similar to the Queen's 25 years later were expressed by a character in George Gissing's novel *In the Year of Jubilee* (1894). It is clear that these were Gissing's own views.

> *Wherever you look now-a-days there's sham and rottenness; but the most worthless creature living is one of these trashy, flashy, girls, – the kind of girl you see everywhere, high and low, – calling themselves 'ladies', – thinking themselves too good for any honest, womanly work. Town and country, it's all the same. They're educated; oh yes, they're educated! What sort of wives do they make, with their education? What sort of mothers are they? Before long, there'll be no such thing as a home. They don't know what the word means. They'd like to live in hotels, and trollop about the streets day and night ... It is astounding to me that they don't get their necks wrung.*

Like Queen Victoria's letter, this passage is very revealing of its author's attitudes. Notice the reference to 'honest, womanly work': what kind of work do you think the writer had in mind? Notice also the last two sentences: these tell us a lot about how the writer regarded women.

Views like these were not surprising in a society that had always been organised in the interests of men. Women in the 18th and early 19th centuries had few legal rights. Unable to vote, unable (if married) to own property, women were treated in law as if they were someone else's possession. They did not even have legal control of their own children, – who remained the property of their fathers.

The first attempts to improve the lot of women in the second half of the 19th century concentrated on strengthening their legal position. Measures such as the Married Women's Property Acts of 1870 and 1882, allowing women to own property even after marriage, were an important first step in the direction of equal rights. At the same time there was growing agitation for women's suffrage (the right to vote). This culminated in the suffragette movement of the early 20th century which drew attention to the cause of women's suffrage but failed, in the short-term, to achieve its aim. The first of the two assignments in this chapter (19.1) looks at the suffragette movement. It focuses in particular on Sylvia Pankhurst, one of the suffragrette leaders, and on the contribution she made to the struggle for equal rights.

In the 20th century war has had a major impact on British society – not least on the position of women. In order to fight the kind of total war that Britain experienced twice in this century governments had to mobilise all the resources of the country. This involved using women to do jobs that would normally have been reserved for men. Whether this led to permanent changes in the position of women is something about which historians disagree. The second of the two assignments in this chapter (19.2) introduces you to the views of some of these historians as well as to the evidence upon which their arguments are based.

One of the interesting things about this topic is that it is still a subject of great controversy today. Studying the role of women in earlier periods introduces you to issues that are still important in the late 20th century. It also makes you think about your own attitudes and the reasons why you have them.

Assignment 18.1
Sylvia Pankhurst, suffragette

Source A
From a biography of Sylvia Pankhurst published by her son Richard Pankhurst in 1979

Sylvia, the artist and Socialist, was by no means convinced that the road to women's **emancipation** lay through the type of organised violence favoured by her mother, elder sister and several other leading Suffragettes. "I believed, then as always," she afterwards wrote, "that the movement required, not more serious militancy by the few, but a stronger appeal to the great masses to join the struggle." Despite this conviction she felt unable to oppose the trend. "I would rather have died at the stake", she wrote, "than say one word against the actions of those who were **in the throes of** the fight ... I realised how supremely difficult is the holding of calm thought and the sense of perspective at such a time..."

emancipation: freedom
in the throes of: in the middle of

In studying economic and social history you have probably noticed how much of the time you are learning about large groups of people: about middle-class women or working-class children or agricultural labourers. An important part of studying history is finding out what these groups had in common. Equally important is finding out how they differed. Don't forget that all groups consist of individuals and that individuals behave in all sorts of different ways. This assignment is designed to show you how one of the leading figures in the early 20th century women's movement was always very much an individual – with her own way of life and her own distinctive views.

Sylvia Pankhurst (1882 – 1960) is less well known than either her mother Emmeline or her elder sister Christabel. All three women, together with another daughter Adela, were active members of the Women's Social and Political Union (WSPU), founded by Emmeline Pankhurst in 1903. They were leaders of the militant wing of the women's movement. It was their belief that only direct action would convince the government that women were serious in demanding the vote. The suffragettes of the WSPU chained themselves to railings, broke windows, dug up golf courses, and heckled cabinet ministers. Many ended up in prison, where they often went on hunger strike and were forcibly fed.

Although one of the organisers of the WSPU, Sylvia Pankhurst's views were in some ways very different from those of other suffragettes. They were also different from those of other members of her own family.

Source B

A cartoon published in 1911 in a suffragette newspaper. The WSPU, emblem used in the cartoon was designed by Sylvia Pankhurst.

THE COMING TOTAL ECLIPSE OF THE ANTI-SUFFRAGISTS.

"It is the duty of the National League for Opposing Woman Suffrage to stir up people from their apathy . . . there is very great risk that the Conciliation Bill will be rushed through Parliament . . ."

—Lord Cromer.

Source C

Sylvia Pankhurst writing about her work among poor women in the East End of London before 1914 (from her book *The Suffragette Movement*, published in 1931)

> I wanted to rouse these women of the submerged mass to be ... fighters on their own account... revolting against the hideous conditions about them, and demanding for themselves and their families a full share in the benefits of civilisation and progress.

Source D

A photograph showing Sylvia Pankhurst addressing a crowd outside the newly opened suffragette headquarters in the East End of London, 1912

Source E

From a letter by Sylvia Pankhurst to Asquith, the Prime Minister, June 1914. Asquith had refused to receive a delegation of women from the East End.

Do you realise that since I was arrested ... I have spoken at dozens of immense public meetings when liable to re-arrest by the police; and in each case the general public, who have come quite freely ... into the largest halls of those districts, have rallied round me, to a man and to a woman, to protect me from the police, although they have incurred many hard blows and risked imprisonment in doing so?

I regard this deputation as of such importance that I have determined, should you refuse to receive the deputation and I be snatched away from the people, as I probably shall be, and taken back to Holloway, my "Cat and Mouse" licence having expired, I will not merely hunger strike in Holloway, as I have done eight times under this present sentence, but when I am released, I shall continue my strike at the door of the Strangers' Entrance to the House of Commons, and shall not take either food or water until you agree to receive this deputation ... although it may end in my death.

Activities

1 Study Source A.

(i) Explain in your own words what is meant by 'militancy'.

(ii) What did Sylvia Pankhurst think about the militant tactics adopted by other suffragettes? Refer to Source A in support of your answer.

(iii) What do you learn from Source A about Sylvia as a person?

2 Study Source B.

(i) Explain in your own words the message of this cartoon.

(ii) What was Sylvia Pankhurst trying to suggest by her drawing on the WSPU emblem?

3 Study Sources C, D and E. What do you learn from Sources C, D and E about the tactics used by Sylvia Pankhurst in support of the women's movement?

4 Complete the following table. The purpose of the exercise is to get you to think about the ways in which Sources C, D and E support what you learn in Source A about Sylvia Pankhurst.

Source A	Source C	Source D	Source E
(a) Sylvia Pankhurst's socialist views	encourages poor to revolt against 'hideous conditions'	....	....
(b)			
(c)			
(d)			

5 Using these sources and any background knowledge you might have, write a short biography of Sylvia Pankhurst (to 1918), showing in particular the contribution she made to the suffragette movement. A biography is an account of a person's life written by someone else.

Assignment 18.2
The effect of the Second World War on the position of women

Historians do not just tell stories about the past. They also try to find patterns in the events they are studying. When they have found these patterns they try to explain them. One important pattern that historians have noticed in 20th century British history is the growth in the number of women with jobs outside the home. Historians also point to the ways in which many jobs that had been previously reserved for men were gradually opened up to women as well. No-one disagrees that this is what happened – the pattern is clear – but they do disagree about *why* it happened. That is the purpose of this assignment – to get you to look at how different historians have explained this pattern and to compare their views with some of the evidence from the time.

Source A
A young married woman training in a government training centre to be a skilled aircraft fitter

Source B
A fashion show in 1942. The purpose of the show was to demonstrate ways in which women's clothes could be made in the simplest posible way, using the least amount of material.

Source C
An advertisement from the early years of the war

In the world-wide unemployment of the 1930s, women had little hope of improving their job prospects, but the Second World War gave them a second chance. This time their importance was such that, like men, they were not asked, but forced to help: Britain, alone in the world, conscripted women into the armed forces or into some other kind of war work. After the war, women continued to work in every conceivable kind of job, until in 1965 about fifty per cent of women aged between fifteen and fifty-nine were in employment – at the end of the First World War, it was only thirty-two per cent.

Source D

From D. C. Brooks, *The Emancipation of Women*, London, 1970

Source E

From Angus Calder, *The People's War*, London, 1969

In conscripting women, Britain went further than any other nation – further than Stalin's Russia and far further than Hitler's Germany...

Yet, as so often with features of wartime life which evoked cries of horror or admiration from contemporaries, what had happened, above all, was the exaggeration of peacetime trends. Certain of the lighter industries – the northern textile mills were the best known example – had long relied on women for half or more of their labour force. Nearly five and a half million women had been in employment before the First World War, which had raised the figure to seven and a half million. Afterwards, a great proportion had left the factories as swiftly as they had invaded them, but a slow rise had been resumed in the 'twenties and 'thirties.

In mid-1943... nearly three million married women and widows were employed, as compared with a million and a quarter before the war. It was calculated that, among those between eighteen and forty, nine single women out of ten and eight married women out of ten were in the forces or in industry...

It was estimated, however, that if peacetime trends had continued without any assistance from Hitler, about six and three-quarter million women would have had jobs outside the home in 1943. Since the official estimate of those employed stood at around seven and a half millions, the number of extra women who were working was no more than about three-quarters of a million – a considerable, but hardly an overwhelming, figure.

Source F

From Arthur Marwick, *World War II*, The Open University, 1973

There is in fact no complete change of social attitudes in the war years. As newsreels and propaganda films bring out... the entry of women into many occupations was considered unusual, frequently the new jobs undertaken were very much along traditional lines, and there was great and continuing stress on the importance of fashion, and great weight was placed on the value of pin-ups as a booster to morale in the forces. It is wrong, then to see a swing of attitude and opinion in one direction... It is equally wrong to ignore the basic economic and social facts of the situation ... Before the war it was common practice in many professions to sack women as soon as they were married. During the war scarcity of labour inevitably meant that married women were given employment ... A survey conducted among various employers at the end of the war showed a considerable swing in opinion with regard to the question of the employment of married women. Of course, many married women, dependent on the miserable allowance paid to soldiers, were badly off: but in general the war meant a new economic and social freedom for women, the experience of which could never be entirely lost.

Activities

1 Which effects of the Second World War on women are illustrated by Source A?

2 Which effects of the Second World War on women are illustrated by Source B?

3 Are the war's effects on women suggested by Source B less important than those suggested by Source A? Give reasons for your answer.

4 Study Source C.

(i) Explain briefly, in your own words, the message of this advertisement.

(ii) What do you learn from this advertisement about people's attitudes towards the position of women?

(iii) Does this advertisement suggest that the war led to major changes in the position of women in society? Explain your answer.

5 Study Sources D, E and F.

(i) What do each of these three authors think about the effects of the Second World War on the position of women in Britain? Comment on each author in turn, supporting your answer by reference to the source.

(ii) Which of the three authors thinks that the Second World War had the biggest impact on women? Explain your answer.

6 (i) Does Source A support Source D? Give reasons for your answer.

(ii) Does Source B support Source E? Give reasons for your answer.

(iii) Which of Sources D, E and F does Source C best support? Give reasons for your answer.

Further activities

1 (i) Make notes on the position of women in Britain at *two* of the following times: 1750; 1900; 1945; 1990. Organise your notes under the following headings: legal rights; involvement in political life; the position of women in the home; educational opportunities; women and jobs.

(ii) Compare the position of women at the two times you have chosen. In what ways had the position of women changed between the two dates and in what ways had it remained the same?

2 Write a short biography of *one* of the following women, showing the ways in which her work helped to bring about changes in the position of women in Britain: Mary Wollstonecraft; Frances Buss; Florence Nightingale; Elizabeth Garrett Anderson; Marie Stopes.

3 How would you explain the following figures taken from a report issued in 1964 by the National Council for Civil Liberties?

- Law: 103 practising women barristers out of a total of 2073
- *Accountants*: 11 000 chartered accountants, 82 of them women
- *Dentists*: 1446 women out of 16 279
- *Finance and Commerce*: 850 women out of 40 574 members of the Institute of Directors

4 Make a study of *one* edition of a newspaper or magazine published before 1970. How useful is this as a source for someone studying the position of women at that time? Support your answer by detailed reference to the source.

5 Study *either* a group of 19th and 20th century paintings in an art gallery, *or* a museum collection of objects relating to home life during the last 200 years. What do you learn from these sources about the position of women or about attitudes towards women during those years?

19 *Britain: A Multicultural Society*

Since the 1960s people have often talked about Britain as a 'multicultural society'. By this they mean a society with many different cultures or ways of life. Some people seem to think that Britain has only become a multicultural society since 1945, as a result of the arrival of large numbers of immigrants from the West Indies and the Indian subcontinent. This is not so.

In fact there were many different cultures in Britain long before the 20th century. To begin with, Britain itself consists of a number of countries each with its distinctive way of life. Scotland and Wales, for example, have their own customs and traditions, a different form of Christianity, and (in the case of Scotland) even different laws. In the 19th century mainland Britain also received large numbers of Irish immigrants, people hoping for a better way of life or trying to escape starvation in their own country. Irish communities were often set apart from the rest of British society, both because of their Roman Catholic religion and because of a different lifestyle.

In addition Britain had always been a refuge for Europeans, such as French Protestants in the 17th century, escaping from religious or political persecution. At the end of the 19th century and in the early years of the 20th century immigration of this kind occurred on a large scale with the arrival of about 100 000 eastern European Jews fleeing from persecution in the Russian Empire.

Until the second half of the 20th century there had been far fewer immigrants from other parts of the world, though even in the 18th century there were small numbers of people of Asian and African descent in many cities. Most had come to Britain either as seamen or as domestic servants.

Britain had therefore always been a multicultural society in one form or another – though it certainly became much more of one after 1945. The purpose of the assignments in this chapter is to help you investigate the development of this multicultural society. The first assignment (19.1) examines Jewish immigration at the end of the 19th century. The second assignment (19.2) looks at one attempt to tackle the problem of racial discrimination.

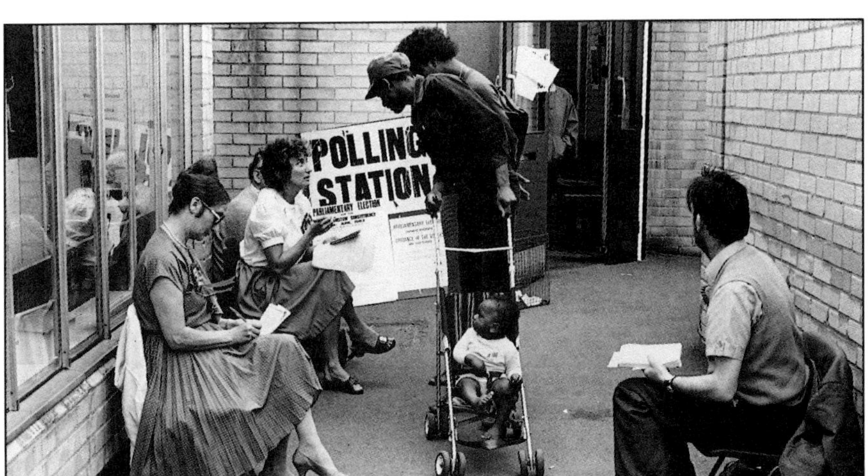

Scene outside a polling station, 1983

Assignment 19.1
Jewish immigrants in late 19th century Britain

After their expulsion from their homeland (Palestine) in the 1st century AD, Jews had settled all over Europe, North Africa and the Middle East (and indeed beyond). Wherever they went they managed to keep many of their old customs and especially their religion and their belief that they were God's chosen people. There had been Jews in England in the early Middle Ages, though very few during the period between 1290 (when they were expelled) and 1664 (when they were officially allowed to return). From the 17th to the mid-19th century most Jews in England were Sephardi Jews from southern Europe, though there were also groups of Ashkenazi Jews from central and eastern Europe as well. By 1850 there were approximately 35 000 Jews altogether, most of them involved in financial dealings of one kind or another. Though tolerated, Jews who practised their religion were denied some of the rights of other British subjects, being unable for example to become members of parliament.

This assignment looks at the big growth in the Jewish community that took place during the period between the mid-1860s and 1905. This growth was caused by the arrival of large numbers of Ashkenazi Jews escaping from persecution in Russian Poland. Approximately 100 000 came to Britain during these years, most of them working-class and desperately poor. The newcomers mostly moved into the same group of occupations: tailoring, boot and shoe making, and the furniture, fur and jewellery trades. As with earlier Jewish immigrants, most came to London where they settled in the East End and especially in Stepney. Large communities were also established in places such as Manchester and Leeds.

This assignment helps you to examine the attitudes of British people (including Jews already settled in the country) towards this immigration. It also helps you find out about the experiences of the immigrants themselves.

Source A
A street inhabited by Jews in the East End of London, 1905

Source B
From a letter to eastern European rabbis, written in 1888 by Nathan Adler, former Chief Rabbi of England. A rabbi is a Jewish religious leader.

... (many of the unfortunate immigrants) who have come here to seek rest ... are lost without livelihoods ... it is difficult for them to support themselves and their households, and at times they ***contravene*** *the will of their Maker on account of poverty and overwork, and* ***violate*** *the* ***Sabbath and Festivals****. Some have been ensnared in the net of the missionaries and renounced their religion, may the Merciful save. Woe to the eyes which see and to the ears which hear such things.*

... it is impossible, for one city cannot support all the refugees of other countries, besides the poor who already reside in it. There are many who believe that all the cobblestones of London are precious stones, and that it is the place of gold. Woe and alas, it is not so ...

(I beg) every rabbi of a community kindly to preach in the ***synagogue*** *and house of study, to publicize the evil which is befalling our brethren who have come here, and to warn them not to come to the land of Britain ...*

contravene: go against
violate the Sabbath and Festivals: work on Jewish holy days. The Sabbath or Saturday is the Jewish holy day of the week.
synagogue: Jewish place of worship

Source C
From a report by J. B. Lakeman, Superintendent Inspector of Workshops in London, 1894

(I am) sorry to chronicle the fact that many Jews, who twelve months ago were strictly orthodox in their religion, have been compelled under penalty of losing their trade to work during their Sabbath, because the Christian (i.e. the West End) employer requires his work to be completed not later than four o'clock on Saturdays.

Source D
From a book by an immigrant rabbi in Liverpool, published in 1919

In the first place, the decision when to work and how many hours of the day to work does not lie in the worker's hand ... if they (the Jewish employers) demand nothing less than to work on the Sabbath, it forces the Jewish worker, who had wanted to rest on the Sabbath, to work ... On the other hand, the Jewish worker was also ashamed, and afraid to make his Jewishness too conspicuous (by objecting).

Source E
From the *Eastern Argus*, a Conservative newspaper, 1887

A number of destitute men and women ... land on our wave-beaten shores in a destitute condition, and offer to do work at any price ... (This) undermines all our commercial arrangements and drives English labour out of the labour market. All the "**sweating system**" in the East of London is carried on by cheap foreign labour.

sweating system: people working long hours in workshops for low pay (also known as 'sweated labour')

Source F
From the *East London Advertiser*, 1899

People of any other nation, after being in England for a short time, **assimilate** themselves with the native race and by and by lose nearly all their foreign trace, but the Jews never do. A Jew is always a Jew. No doubt this is due to their desire for the formation of a new Hebrew nation, a fact which inclines them to look upon themselves as pilgrims in a strange land.

assimilate: adopt the way of life of

Source G
From the *Jewish Chronicle*, 1888

If poor Jews will persist in **appropriating** whole streets to themselves in the same district, if they will ... persevere ... in congregating in a body at prominent points in a great public thoroughfare like the Whitechapel or Commercial Road, drawing (attention) to their peculiarities of dress, of language and of manner ... can there be any wonder that the **vulgar prejudices** should be kept alive and strengthened?

appropriating: taking over
the vulgar prejudices:the prejudices of ordinary (or 'vulgar') people

Activities

1 Study Source A.

(i) 'Desperately poor and often living in conditions of great squalor'. Does Source A support this statement about Jewish immigrants in the East End of London? Comment carefully on the photograph in support of your answer.

(ii) What are the problems of using photographs as evidence when studying social history? Illustrate your answer by reference to Source A.

2 Study Source B.

(i) What reasons does Nathan Adler give for advising eastern European Jews 'not to come to the land of Britain'?

(ii) Do you think that Adler's account of conditions among immigrant Jews is likely to be a reliable one? Give reasons for your answer.

3 (i) What do you learn from Sources B, C and D about the reasons why some immigrant Jews worked on the Sabbath?

(ii) Is there any way of knowing which of these reasons was the main reason why some immigrant Jews worked on the Sabbath? Explain your answer.

4 (i) What criticisms are made of Britain's Jewish community by Sources E and F?

(ii) Why do you think these criticisms were made?

5 (i) Does Source G make the same criticisms as Sources E and F? Refer to the sources in support of your answer.

(ii) Which section of the Jewish community is most likely to have agreed with Source G? Explain your answer.

6 Write a short account of *one* of the following, showing its importance in the development of Britain's Jewish communities: the Aliens Act of 1905; anti-semitism in Britain during the inter-war years; Mosley's British Union of Fascists and the East End of London; Jewish refugees from Nazi Germany during the 1930s; the way of life of Britain's Jewish communities during the 20th century.

Assignment 19.2
Was the Race Relations Act of 1968 necessary and was it effective?

Since 1945 four main groups of immigrants have arrived in Britain: east–Europeans, such as Poles, escaping from the communist states that were established after the end of the Second World War; West Indians; people of Asian descent from the former British colonies of the Indian subcontinent and east Africa; and the Irish. The largest of these groups was the Irish.

Immigration became a major political issue during these years. Concern in some quarters about the immigration of large numbers of people of non-European descent led both Conservative and Labour governments to introduce restrictions on immigration. These restrictions were often bitterly attacked – both for going too far and for not going far enough.

At the same time as restricting immigration, governments also turned their attention to the problem of race relations. Many people of non-European descent found that they were discriminated against on grounds of race. A series of Race Relations Acts – in 1965, 1968 and 1976 – have attempted to tackle this problem. This assignment looks at one of these acts, at what it was trying to do and at the different opinions that people had about it.

Source A
From *The Sunday Times*, 23 April 1967

If the law does not guarantee a coloured immigrant's right to a job for which he is qualified and a home for which he can pay no one else will... Left to the ... guidance of their own fears and suspicions, too many employers, union leaders, landlords, estate agents and credit merchants do not and will not regard a coloured man as the equal of a white.

Source B
From the *Yorkshire Post*, 27 July 1967

The latest dose of well meaning foolishness from the Home Office would extend **the Act** to deal with discrimination on grounds of colour, race or ethnic or national origins in employment, housing, insurance and credit facilities. Discrimination on those grounds alone in any of these fields is wicked and uncivilised but we doubt whether it happens as much as people are being led to imagine it does. The trouble is that immigrants are being encouraged to believe that the factors which discriminate against sections of the native population (such as lack of qualifications for the job, the absence of guarantees for credit facilities or housing, and the high fire risk in overcrowded houses) do not apply to them. They are being encouraged to believe that if they are asked to leave a first-class railway seat when they have only a second-class ticket it is because of their colour.

the Act: *the Race Relations Act of 1965*

Source C

From Louis Kushnick, *British Anti-Discrimination Legislation*, 1971

The (1968) Act extends the areas in which discrimination on the grounds of colour, race, or ethnic or national origins is made unlawful, to include employment, housing, credit and insurance facilities, education, and all places of public resort including shops and offices ... It **exempts** employment in private households and on merchant ships where the sharing of sleeping or mess facilities would follow from the ending of discrimination. It exempts for the first two years employers of 25 or fewer employees; in the second two years, employers of 10 or fewer employees will be exempted, after which time the Act will cover all employers except for those exempted by the provisions mentioned above.

In the housing field ... there will be **a phased implementation** of the provisions, with shared accommodation involving fewer than 12 persons in addition to the landlord and his family being exempt for the first two years, and with a permanent exemption for shared accommodation involving six or fewer persons thereafter.

The size of the Race Relations Board is to be expanded to twelve persons and it will be empowered to initiate investigations where it has reason to suspect that discrimination has occurred.

exempts: does not include
a phased implementation: being introduced gradually (in phases)

Source D

From John Rex and Sally Tomlinson, *Colonial Immigrants in a British City*, London, 1979

In the face of (the) discrimination and segregation which exists, the activities of the Race Relations Board, within the terms of the 1968 Act, have been little less than **derisory** ... (One researcher) estimates, on the basis of his tests, that some 6,000 cases of discrimination must occur (each year) in the field of unskilled employment alone ... Given the actual scale of the problem of immigrant disadvantage, it seems clear that the Race Relations Act of 1968 is making no significant difference.

derisory: laughable

Source E

Complaints received under the Race Relations Act of 1968, during the period April 1969–March 1970

Type	Total number	Opinion: discrimination	Opinion: no discrimination
EMPLOYMENT COMPLAINTS			
Recruitment	202	21	181
Terms	43	1	42
Conditions	47	2	45
Training	4	0	4
Promotion	28	3	25
Dismissal	176	7	169
Trades Unions	11	1	10
Advertisements	37	32	5
COMPLAINTS OTHER THAN EMPLOYMENT			
Public places	–	–	–
Public houses and hotels	64	31	33
Clubs	8	4	4
Public transport	4	2	2
Other	20	9	11
GOODS, FACILITIES/AND SERVICES			
Insurance: motor	8	5	3
Insurance: other	3	0	3
Financial and credit facilities	12	0	12
Education: facilities	12	1	11
Education: grants	11	0	11
Services connected with employment	18	2	16
Social services	9	0	9
Medical services	14	0	14
Other	46	2	44
Private housing (rent)	36	4	32
Private housing (sale)	5	3	2
Estate agents	32	3	29
Public housing	12	2	10
Advertisements	116	111	5

Activities

1 Study Sources A and B.

(i) Which of these sources is supporting the introduction of a new Race Relations Act and which is opposing it?

(ii) Explain in your own words what is meant by racial discrimination.

(iii) Sources A and B make different claims about the effects of making racial discrimination illegal. Describe these claims in your own words.

(iv) How would you try to find out whether or not these claims were correct?

2 Study Source C. Why did parliament include in the 1968 Act the various exemptions listed in this source?

3 Study Sources D and E.

(i) Does Source E suggest that there was far more discrimination in employment than in any other aspect of life? Refer in detail to the tables in support of your answer.

(ii) In which aspect of life did the Race Relations Board uphold most of the complaints? How would you explain this?

(iii) Does Source E support Source D? Explain your answer.

4 What further measures have been taken to combat racial discrimination in Britain during the 1970s and 1980s, and with what success?

Further activities

1 Choose *one* ethnic minority in modern Britain (an 'ethnic minority' is a group of people who are not of British descent). Write a short history of this ethnic minority in Britain, organising your answer under these headings: when and why this minority came to Britain; where they settled; the way of life of this minority in Britain (e.g. employment, customs, etc); relations between this minority and other groups; the impact of this ethnic minority on British society.

Possible ethnic minorities which you might choose include: Poles; Ukrainians; Irish; West Indians; West Africans; Indians; Pakistanis; Bangladeshis; Chinese; Italians; Lithuanians; Cypriots; Latin Americans.

2 Compare the experiences of *two* different ethnic minorities in either 19th or 20th century Britain. What similarities and what differences do you notice between these experiences?

3 Conduct *two* interviews with people who have been living in Britain for many years, but who were born in another country of non-British parents. Compare the experiences of these two people with regard to (a) reasons for coming to Britain, (b) feelings about Britain at the time of arrival, and (c) feelings about Britain since arrival. How would you explain any differences between the experiences of these two people?

4 How would you explain the racial prejudice that has often been present in Britain during the 19th and 20th centuries?